SERIOUSLY
SIMPLE

Matador
9 De Montfort Mews
Leicester LE1 7FW, UK
Tel: (+44) 116 255 9311 / 9312
Email: books@troubador.co.uk
Web: www.troubador.co.uk/matador

Matador is an imprint of Troubador Publishing

ISBN 1 904744 98 2

Cover illustration: © Photos.com

Typeset in 11pt American Typewriter by Troubador Publishing Ltd, Leicester, UK
Printed by The Cromwell Press Ltd, Trowbridge, Wilts, UK

SERIOUSLY SIMPLE

IF YOU CAN READ...
YOU CAN COOK

Bidi Jones

CONTENTS

INTRODUCTION

COOKING might seem terrifying if you have never done it before, but I think **if you can READ** an easy recipe, **you can COOK** – if you really want to. You don't need the skills of a top chef to make great tasting, healthy food.

If you've never cooked before – then this is the book for you, because the recipes have been made as easy as possible and, in addition, they have the enormous benefit of doing what all inexperienced cooks find difficult, namely, getting everything ready to eat at the same time. Unless you have experience, you don't know when to put on the potatoes, vegetables or rice, or how long these things will take to cook. With these recipes this has all been worked out for you. With all the main meal recipes you should be able to start at the beginning, follow the recipes, add a piece of fruit and end up with a complete meal on the table.

Just follow the simple instructions, and with most of the recipes (not the sweet things or soups) you get the basis of a whole meal, tasty and nutritious. Give it a go!

This book is about good, home cooked, everyday food. Not fancy cuisine. There is plenty of time for that later. The recipes have been carefully created to both taste good and let you eat healthily.

Use it for a while and cooking should seem more familiar. If you learn your skills with these easy recipes then you can branch out, adapt and create your own meals.

When you feel confident with the basics and want to be a bit more adventurous, you can find some other sources of food information. The public library has shelves full of books, both of recipes and on nutrition. The internet has lots of food related sites.

Follow the Healthy Eating advice given and you will not go far wrong.

One of the real advantages of cooking for yourself is that you can choose what you eat. And probably more importantly, you choose what not to

THE MINIMUM SKILLS NEEDED TO USE THIS BOOK ARE

1. Cut safely onto a board
2. Follow hygiene and safety instructions
3. Use an oven
4. Cope with boiling liquids
5. Follow a recipe
6. Open tins

eat. You are in control, not at the mercy of advertisers.

Why not just get a takeaway? The main reason is that "You are what you eat", and this way you decide what you eat. Takeaways are usually fairly tasty, but frequently they are not good nutritionally as they contain too much fat and salt, and don't provide an adequate long-term diet. A few bad meals do you no harm, but a lifetime of them does your health no favours at all, and the long-term consequences can be very serious. A good diet has proven health benefits.

It's up to you what you eat. If you don't like what is on offer at midday, don't buy a bag of chips – make yourself a sandwich. You can make it the night before, wrap it in clingfilm and store it in the fridge. Use wholemeal bread, add some protein, such as cooked meat, cheese, egg, fish, and add some salad, lettuce, cucumber or tomato. You're getting there nutritionally. Or make a salad in a box and take a wholemeal roll to eat with it. Pack it in an insulated container. Take a drink of fruit juice, milk or water and there you are – cheaper and healthier.

Why don't you consider offering to make a meal for everyone in your household once a week? Most people are more than pleased if someone offers to make supper for everyone occasionally. Especially if they clean the kitchen up after them...

Cooking can be fun. I know of a group who meet once a month to have a meal together. Each person takes it in turn to prepare one part of the meal. They are very creative in finding new ideas. For them it has been a great way to make new friends in a new city.

If money is short, don't cut down on a balanced diet, but consider beans, lentils, cheese and eggs as protein. Stewing meats are much cheaper than frying or grilling cuts, and slow cooking in a casserole with vegetables brings out a wonderful flavour. Buy fresh vegetables when they are in season – they are much cheaper then.

For new cooks, frozen vegetables do make the job easier, faster and less stressful. It is much easier to "get a result". There is plenty of time to improve techniques, and increase knowledge later. Starting cooking is what matters. I really think it is much better to cut a few corners than to make things too difficult and discouraging.

As the emphasis is on **easy** in these recipes, everything is simplified as far as possible. Some experienced cooks think this is a bit unorthodox, but the testers liked the results, and that's what matters.

There aren't many sweet things. I think that fruit or yoghourt are better for you, but my young testers said I was mean. They said they enjoyed making buns and cakes, and anyway, that is how they first started cooking, aged about 3. They won. So there are a few.

KITCHEN HYGIENE AND SAFETY: A BRIEF INTRODUCTION

Kitchens are full of hazards. You will not be popular if you burn the place down, injure yourself or poison everyone...

BE CLEAN
- Wash your hands before cooking and after touching meat or fish.
- Wash up in hot water and detergent and have clean tea towels.
- Wash all boards and utensils which have been used for meat and fish very thoroughly.
- Rinse meat (not mince) and fish under running water.
- Keep animals out of the kitchen and off the work surfaces.
- Cover cuts with waterproof sticking plaster.
- Do not touch mouth, nose or hair while cooking. Long hair should be tied back.

- Keep work surfaces clean

SEPARATE
- Separate raw and cooked meats when cooking.
- Have separate chopping boards for raw and cooked meats
- Separate raw and cooked meats in the fridge. Raw meat should go in the bottom so that blood cannot drip onto other food.
- Cover food in the fridge.

DON'T
- Don't eat mouldy food, except blue cheese which is within date limit.
- Don't eat food that smells or tastes "off".
- Don't have trailing electric cords in the kitchen.

DO
- Observe "use by" dates

FOOD STORAGE
- Don't leave leftover food in tins. Put into ceramic, glass or plastic containers. Cover and put in fridge.
- Foods that are purchased chilled in the shop should be kept in a refrigerator at home, and not allowed to get warm on the way back from the shop.
- Check "use by" dates are not exceeded.
- Do not put hot food straight into the fridge. Cool as quickly as possible. Cover and then refrigerate.
- If the label says "refrigerate after opening", do so.
- Don't let leftovers stay in the fridge for more than a day or so. They might become a health hazard.
- If reheating food, make sure it is piping hot right through.
- Frozen food should not be re-frozen once defrosted and should be eaten soon after being de-frosted.
- Do not store raw and cooked meats together in the fridge. Do not let blood drip onto other foods.

- Read and observe dates on frozen food.

- Be aware of storage advice given on labels.

HEALTHY EATING

This is an enormously complex subject. This is only a very brief start.

A doctor once told me, "You will have a healthy diet if you have food of several different bright colours, red. green, orange etc. on your plate." This is not the whole story, but it's a pretty good start.

To maintain health a body needs a balance of

- **VEGETABLES AND FRUIT**. Each day eat at least five portions of fruit and vegetables. Green vegetables (broccoli, sprouts, green beans, cabbage etc) and red and yellow fruit and vegetables (carrots, sweet potatoes, peppers, tomatoes oranges, mangoes etc) are very important. Do not overcook green vegetables, or they will lose some of their vitamins. Try to include some unsalted nuts or seeds, such as cashews or sunflower seeds. Vegetables and fruit should be a very important part of your diet.

- **CARBOHYDRATES** are found in bread, pasta, cereals, potatoes, rice, sugar and some vegetables. Carbohydrates give energy. Wholegrain carbohydrate foods are not heavily processed and so they contain more nutrients and fibre than processed white flour products. Wholegrain foods should be a major part of your diet. Wholemeal bread is a better choice than white bread..

- **PROTEIN** is found mainly in meat, fish, eggs, cheese, beans, lentils, Quorn and Tofu. Protein is essential for healthy body tissues such as skin, hair, and muscles.

- **FAT** is found mainly in oil and animal fat. Oils, such as corn or olive are best. Cut fat off meat. Use all fats and oils sparingly.

- **DAIRY FOODS**. Low fat milk, yoghourt, and a small amount of cheese will give your body the calcium which it needs for strong bones.

A diet containing all of these should provide the nourishment the body needs to be healthy.

DO

- Wash all fruit and vegetables before eating. Cook green vegetables until only just tender, to preserve the vitamins.

- Cut down on salt. Don't shake it over your meal. Remember processed meals contain a lot of salt.

- Cut down on sugar. Avoid hidden sugar in processed foods and fizzy drinks

- Cut down on fats in general and saturated fats in particular. Saturated fats are often hard at room temperature, like butter or meat fat. Use oils such as olive, corn, soy etc. Choose skimmed or semi skimmed milk and low fat yoghourt. There is a lot of hidden saturated fat in chocolate bars, cakes and processed meals.

- Learn to read the contents list on packets.

- Eat breakfast. Wholemeal toast or wholewheat cereal, (read the packet to check for hidden sugar) with low fat milk will give a good start to the day. Also eat a piece of fruit, or have a glass of fruit juice. Consider making porridge. It doesn't take long and is filling and cheap.

NOTES ON THE RECIPES   Recipes serve four!

GETTING EVERYTHING ORGANISED BEFORE YOU BEGIN

Assembling and weighing all the ingredients before beginning makes the job much easier. I totally recommend it.

WHY THE RECIPES ARE WRITTEN IN THE WAY THEY ARE

Because the recipes in this book make all the parts of the entire main course of a meal, (which most cookery books do not) they are laid out in an unusual manner. Just add fruit or yoghourt to complete the meal.

The notes below explain the reasons for the order of the step by step instructions.

1. *Very often the first instructions in a recipe are for the preparation of things that will be used later in the recipe.*

    This ensures that everything will be on hand when it is time for it to be added to the cooking and there will not be any holdups for something to be washed and cut up or peeled.

    For example

    > Wash and chop the coriander.
    > Rinse the lentils.

    This means, do the task, and set it aside. It will be needed further on in the recipe.

2. *Please read through the whole recipe before beginning.*

    Often, while one part of the dish is cooking, another part is also being prepared. The underlined text gives you a reminder of when it is necessary to do things quickly.

    For example

    > …<u>as soon as the curry is cooking</u>, start the RICE.

    This is because you are making several things at the same time, and the recipe is organized so that you end up with everything finished together.

3. *Whenever a new part of the recipe is being started, capital letters are used to indicate a major change.*

    For example

    > cook the VEGETABLES

    It may look a bit odd, but a lot of different things are being co-ordinated and the different parts have to slot in together so that everything is finished at the same time.

INGREDIENTS

These have been chosen to be easily available.

BAKING PARCHMENT
This is used under cakes to stop them sticking to the tin. Cut it to size from the roll. Greaseproof paper, well oiled, can be used instead.

BEANS (NOT BAKED BEANS)
Tinned beans have been recommended in these recipes because they are quick and easy. Some contain added salt and sugar, which is not ideal. This may make the recipe too salty. If you cannot get beans without added salt, adjust the recipe by leaving out the stock cube, which also contains salt. Drain and rinse the beans before using. Beans are healthy because they contain both protein and fibre and can be used to "stretch" a small amount of meat into a whole meal.

Dried beans are cheaper than tinned, but take a long time to prepare, as they have to be soaked overnight before cooking. They can be cooked in bulk, separated into containers and frozen. Some beans, such as kidney beans, once soaked, have to be boiled fast for 10 minutes, before simmering until cooked. This is to destroy harmful substances in the beans. Read the packets and check the correct cooking procedure

BREAD
Wholemeal bread is healthier than white because it contains more nutrients and fibre, though there are some white loaves which have had

---

MEASURING THE INGREDIENTS

To make measuring easier, as far as possible measurements are given in cups. They are a standard 8 ounce measure. Sets of cups are available in supermarkets.

If you cannot find a set, or do not want to buy one, find a cup or container that holds 8 fluid ounces, and keep that handy to use.

A set of measuring spoons is also very useful.

---

additional nutrients added and are better than regular white bread.

There are many interesting and tasty new varieties of bread available.

COCONUT MILK
Reduced fat coconut milk works fine. I always use it.

CURRY PASTE
These recipes use curry paste. There are several different flavours which vary from strong to mild. Read the jar label for storage instructions. Some curry pastes should be kept in the fridge and have the warning that they should not be consumed uncooked and may contain nuts. Curry paste adds saltiness as well as flavour to a recipe.

Real curry fans may soon want to move on to using individual spices, but the paste is very easy and quick to use.

DAIRY PRODUCTS
Crème fraiche, cream and sour cream are virtually interchangeable when being used to enrich a soup or stew. I always use reduced fat products rather than full fat.

Yoghourt or fromage frais have a tendency to curdle and separate when heated. This doesn't look good but will not affect the taste.

Quark is a very low fat soft cheese, which mixes very well with other ingredients to give a "luxurious" feel, without high fat and calories.

GARLIC
I have tested fresh, frozen and processed in oil in these recipes. I tried Fresh Garlic in Sunflower Oil and was very pleased with the results. Garlic is also sometimes available frozen. I found mine in the organic section of the freezer department of the supermarket.

To prepare fresh garlic, break a clove from the bulb (which consists of several cloves), peel off the outer papery skin, and press into a garlic press or chop very finely.

Don't cook fresh garlic too fiercely or it will burn and the flavour will be spoiled.

IF YOU FANCY MAKING YOUR OWN GARLIC BREAD

Preheat the oven to 200°C (400°F)

2 baguettes
110g (4 oz) soft margarine, or butter, at room temperature
3 cloves of garlic, peeled and crushed

Mix the garlic into the margarine or butter.
Cut the bread into slices, almost through to the base, but not quite.
Spread the margarine or butter evenly into the cuts you have made.
Wrap the baguettes in foil.
Put into the oven for 15 minutes.

Unwrap foil. Serve.
Use oven gloves. Foil will be hot.

GINGER

I tried both Ginger in Sunflower oil and fresh root ginger in these recipes. Both work very well.

Fresh ginger is a brown knobbly root. Buy a smallish piece approximately (10cm or 4"). It will keep in the fridge for several weeks before it becomes shrivelled. To use it, scrape or peel off the outer brown skin and grate or finely chop the root. A length of about 2.5cm(1") is usually about right amount for a recipe. It is possible to grate a larger quantity of ginger root and freeze it in small amounts. If you only want the flavour of the ginger and do not care for the fibrous texture of the root, peel and slice enough to make 4-6 slices. When the food is cooked, remove the ginger slices.

HERBS AND GARNISHES

Pot grown herbs can be bought at a supermarket, but in my experience they seldom have a long life. Those bought at a Farmers' Market usually last well.

I have also tried out frozen chopped herbs, which are fine – if you can get hold of them. They have the additional advantage of always being in the freezer. Again, check out the freezer section of the supermarket.

I get mine from the organic section.

Some herbs such as oregano, mixed herbs, thyme and parsley are frequently used dried to give flavour.

Although fresh and frozen leaf coriander gives a better flavour, freeze dried coriander (green, not dried brown powdered) will do if fresh is not available.

LENTILS

Lentils can be bought both dried and tinned. They provide both protein and fibre. There are many types of lentil, but the dried ones used in this book are red, because they cook quickly.

MEAT

- Never allow raw meat to get in contact with any other ingredients.

- Always wash knives, boards and all utensils used with meat, very thoroughly after use, in detergent and hot water.

- Do not use utensils used with raw meat with any other foodstuffs until they have been washed.

- Store meat covered in the fridge. Do not let it get into contact with other foodstuffs.

GAS MARK TEMPERATURES

I you have a gas stove with a regulo which indicates the temperature, the equivalent temperatures are listed below.

Mark 1	140°C	275°F
Mark 2	150°C	300°F
Mark 3	170°C	325°F
Mark 4	180°C	350°F
Mark 5	190°C	375°F
Mark 6	200°C	400°F
Mark 7	220°C	425°F
Mark 8	230°C	450°F

- Observe the suggestions in the *Kitchen Hygiene and Safety* section p3.

I have tried to find meats that are easy to prepare, inexpensive and that will be freely available in most supermarkets.

At the moment there is a very strong movement towards better animal husbandry and improved qualities of meat. If you want to know more about this, ask a good local butcher or go to your Farmer's Market.

Mince
It is well worth while buying the best possible mince. Aside from any health considerations, cheap mince is very fatty.

Pork
As all the recipes using pork in this book are for pork casseroles, buy either pork chops, or stewing pork. Cut off any fat. Rinse large pieces before using.

Stewing beef
This cooks best in a casserole and if jacket potatoes are cooked at the same time, it is a very easy meal. Buy either ready cut casserole beef, or buy beef for casseroles, such as topside or chuck. Cut off any fat. Rinse large pieces of beef before using.

The very best beef casseroles are slow cooked at 160°C (310°F) for $2\frac{1}{2}$ hours, see *Slow Cooked Beef Casserole*, but this recipe needs fresh vegetables to be prepared and is not suitable for baked potatoes to accompany the meat, which makes it more effort for an inexperienced or busy cook.

Sausages
There is a wide variety of different types available. Buy the best you can afford as they should have a better meat content. Try varying the recipes with different types of sausage.

NUTS
If you have a nut allergy, avoid cooking and eating any recipe containing nuts or peanut oil or any other nut oil. Check the bottle.

OILS
Any good vegetable oil will do such as olive, corn, sunflower, etc.

ONIONS

Frozen onions are the easy option for new and young cooks. They cook quickly and won't make your eyes sting. Just take out what you need, seal the bag up carefully and replace in the freezer. Frozen onions can look a bit "wet" when first put in the pan. They will soon dry off, soften and brown in a few minutes.

However, they are more expensive than going to the local market and buying them loose.

If you are going to use fresh onions they will take a few minutes longer to cook than the frozen, so allow a little more time for the recipe.

If the smell of frying fresh onions is too strong, put a lid on the pan for a few minutes until they have started to cook, when the raw smell will be less strong.

PEPPER

Freshly ground black pepper gives the best results in these recipes.

PINCH OF...

Means just what it says. It's what you can pinch between your finger and thumb. I reckon it is approximately $1/4$ teaspoon.

QUORN

Vegetable protein available in chunks or mince. Absorbs flavour of other ingredients. Can be used as a substitute for meat.

SALADS

Salad does not have to be just lettuce and tomato. Consider adding grated carrot, spinach leaves, watercress, onion, chives, herbs, avocado, peppers, cucumber, courgettes, beetroot, fruit, nuts or seeds, or dried fruit. The list is endless. Or you can do it the easy way (and more expensive) and buy a ready prepared bag.

If you enjoy salads, do some research and find new and exciting recipes. There are dozens out there. Create your own.

Salad dressings are another area you might wish to do some research in. A good dressing can enliven a salad. There are lots of recipes. And again you

EASY SALAD DRESSING

4 tablespoons olive oil. 2 tablespoons of lemon juice, or wine vinegar, cider vinegar or sherry vinegar. 1 teaspoon brown sugar, $1/2$ teaspoon Dijon mustard.

Mix all thoroughly. Season with salt and pepper.
I keep an old, washed, commercial salad dressing bottle to shake it and keep it in. Refrigerate.

could create your own. Or do it the quick way and buy one ready made.

TOFU
Soy bean curd. Very bland in flavour, but is a low fat, low calorie, healthy protein, which is very useful in a strong flavoured dish.

VEGETABLES. FRESH OR FROZEN?
Frozen vegetables are often suggested in these recipes because they save time and there is no waste if the packet is carefully re-sealed and replaced in the freezer speedily. They are processed so fast that the important vitamins are preserved. Above all they are EASY.

Frozen onions are particularly convenient, especially for very young cooks who have trouble coping with their eyes watering when preparing fresh. More varieties of frozen vegetables appear all the time. Diced swede or cabbage would be ideal for adding in small quantities to soups or casseroles. Check out what is available.

Almost all the recipes in this book can be made with fresh vegetables. Extra time must be allowed for their preparation and cooking.

Fresh vegetables in season are always much tastier and also cheaper, which is very important for the budget conscious. And don't forget that adding more vegetables will "stretch" the protein part of the meal, which is also important if you are counting the pennies.

Many vegetables are now available partially prepared, but you will pay for someone else's labour.

Frozen vegetables cook more quickly, but fresh vegetables really have the advantage in long slow cooking, when frozen vegetables tend to lose their shape and break up. Undoubtedly a slowly cooked beef casserole is better with fresh vegetables, but I feel that it is much better to use frozen vegetables than for the cook to feel it is all too much trouble and not attempt to make any food at all.

People have strong likes and dislikes and this is one area where it is very easy to make changes. Cook what you like. Just eat plenty.

I have not included microwave instructions. However vegetables do cook well in a microwave. To cook them follow the instructions on the pack.

Farmer's Markets have some great fruit and vegetables.

PREPARING FRESH VEGETABLES

At the beginning of many of the recipes it says "if you are using fresh vegetables, prepare them now." So here are a few tips.

This is a very brief overview. There are many interesting ways of preparing vegetables, but there isn't space for them here. Lots of packets have instructions on them and if you buy vegetables loose (much cheaper) just follow the general rules.

Remember to allow extra time for the preparation of fresh vegetables.

BROCCOLI AND CAULIFLOWER
Wash well in cold water. Cut out the woody stalk and break the large head into small pieces (florets) Cook in a saucepan with 1 cup water and a pinch of salt. Bring to the boil. Reduce heat and cook, bubbling gently, with a lid on the pan, for approximately 10 minutes until just tender when tested with the point of a knife. Drain by using a colander placed in the sink.

BRUSSELS SPROUTS
Wash in cold water. Cut off the hard base and remove any scruffy outer leaves. Put in a saucepan, add 1 cup of cold water and a pinch of salt. Bring to the boil, then reduce the heat, put a lid on the pan and cook gently bubbling for 10-12 minutes until just tender when tested with the point of a knife. Drain by using a colander placed in the sink.

CABBAGE

Wash in cold water. Pull off any scruffy outer leaves. Cut the cabbage in quarters and cut out the woody core. Check the leaves are clean. Either shred the cabbage downwards onto a board, or roll several leaves up together and slice the roll up finely. Cook as broccoli.

CARROTS AND ALL ROOT VEGETABLES

Peel the carrots with a vegetable peeler then, cutting downwards on a chopping board, slice, dice or cut into pieces.

The recipe in which the carrots are to be used should determine their size. A slow cooking beef casserole can have large pieces, whereas a quickly cooked recipe should have finely diced ones in order that they get wholly cooked.

To cook them as a separate vegetable put them into a saucepan with 1 cup of water and a $1/_2$ teaspoon salt, bring to the boil, reduce the heat, and cook with a lid on the pan, bubbling gently for about 15 minutes. Test with the point of a knife for tenderness.

Root vegetables can be roasted in the oven. Follow the instructions for *Big Chips* (see below).

The skin or peel of some root vegetables, such as some squashes and pumpkin is very tough, and care should be taken when preparing them.

COURGETTES

Wash them in cold water. Trim the ends and slice thinly. Cook as broccoli.

GREEN BEANS

Dwarf beans. Wash and trim the ends. Cut into small pieces and cook in a saucepan with 1 cup of water and a pinch of salt. Bring to the boil. Turn the heat down and cook, gently bubbling, with a lid on the pan, for approximately 10-15 minutes until they are tender when tested with the point of a knife. Drain by using a colander placed in the sink.

Runner beans. If they are not very young and small, pull the "string" from the wider edge of the bean or cut off this edge. They are usually cut thinly on the diagonal. If any bean seems stringy and tough when you cut it, throw it away. Cook as dwarf beans.

LEEKS

Cut off the base root end and the leaf tips and throw away any scruffy outer leaves. Leeks often have dirt in between the green part of the leaves, so I personally separate the leaves and check each for dirt. Then I slice them thinly and cook them as broccoli. This wrecks the elegant shape of the leek but at least there are no crunches of grit.

You can also separate the green part of the leaves, without pulling them right off, clean them well and cook the leeks either whole or sliced lengthways, in bubbling, slightly salted water, for 10-15 minutes until tender when tested with the tip of a knife.

Lightly cooked leeks can be put in an ovenproof dish, white or cheese sauce poured on top and the top browned under the grill or in the oven.

MUSHROOMS

Most instructions say just wipe, but I always rinse them thoroughly in cold water, pick off any bits of soil and cut off the bottom of the stalk. Slice and fry for a few minutes in oil.

They are also very good baked in the oven for 20–30 minutes (depending on size) with a little oil drizzled over. Put them in the oven with a casserole.

ONIONS

Cut off the top and bottom and remove the tough outer skin. Cut the onion in half from top to bottom. Lay one half of the onion flat on a chopping board and slice thinly with a sharp knife. Slice in the opposite direction to make dice.

POTATOES

Boiled (old)
About 225g-275g (8-10oz) per person. Peel and cut medium potatoes into halves and large ones into quarters. Place in a saucepan and just cover with cold water. Add 1 teaspoon salt. Bring to the boil. Then turn down the heat and cook covered, bubbling gently, with a lid on the pan, for about 20 minutes until tender when tested with the point of a knife. Drain by using a colander placed in the sink.

Boiled (new)
About 110g–175g (4–6oz) per person. Wash them in cold water. Place in

saucepan. Just cover with cold water. Add ½ teaspoon salt. Bring to the boil. Then reduce the heat and cook, with a lid on the pan, bubbling gently, for about 15 minutes until tender when tested with the point of a knife. Drain by using a colander placed in the sink.

Mashed
As Boiled(old) above, but they can be cut into smaller pieces. When tender, drain, return to the saucepan and take the potato masher and mash firmly downwards until all the lumps are broken up.

Creamed Mash
As above, but add 25g (1oz) butter or margarine and a little milk and mix with a wooden spoon until smooth.

Mashed potatoes plus. Add any one of the following: fried onion or garlic, grain mustard, horseradish, crisp fried chopped bacon, a pinch of chili, a little Cajun spice, grated cheese, soft cheese - the list is endless. Use your imagination with the things you can easily add to give zing to your mashed potatoes.

Bubble and squeak, usually made by adding cooked cabbage to mashed or creamed potato and fried, can be adapted to add many interesting vegetables. If you have left over mashed potatoes and vegetables you can mix them, make the mixture into small patties, or just fry lightly as a hash, with 1 or 2 tablespoons of oil in the frying pan. Serve with eggs or bacon and a salad for a quick meal.

Jacket
Check for dirt. Cut out any large blemishes. Wash in cold water. Prick the skin with a fork in several places. Preheat the oven to 200°C (400° F) and place the potatoes in for one hour. (If the potatoes are very large they may need longer, up to 1½ hours) Check for tenderness by using the tip of a knife.

Big Chips
Peel about 900g (2lbs) potatoes and cut into big chips. 4 from a normal potato, 8 from a baking potato. Take 3–4 tablespoons of oil and brush each potato all over with the oil. Pour any remaining oil over.

Place in single layer in baking tin. Shake 1 teaspoon of salt over. (or Cajun spices or similar) Bake in an oven preheated to 180°C (350° F) for about 45 minutes, turning at least once.

SALADS

All salad ingredients should be thoroughly washed in cold water. Leafy items should be shaken dry or dried in a salad spinner.

Cut other salad items such as tomatoes, peppers or cucumber into small pieces or slices.

Fruit should be washed, peeled if necessary and cut up.

Carrots should be peeled and grated.

Avocadoes should be peeled and cut up. A ripe avocado should give very slightly when pressed gently.

Beetroot are best when bought fresh and boiled in water. Keep the skin on to cook and do not cut the top and bottom off closely or they will "bleed" during cooking. The cooking time will depend on the age and size. Test with the tip of a knife to see if they are tender. When they are cooked, leave them to cool in the water and peel when cool.

Beetroot can also be bought ready prepared, but this is more expensive and sometimes heavily vinegared.

SWEET PEPPERS (NOT HOT CHILI PEPPERS) RED, GREEN, YELLOW

Wash very thoroughly. Cut in half and remove the seeds. Cut on a board into whatever size the recipe needs.

Can be oven roasted, following the *Big Chips* method above.

I think the last word here belongs to the wonderful great, great grand-mother of Luthien. (Luthien makes a great flapjack, try it in the Sweet Things section.) As a young bride, in about 1900, she was asked how she would cook for her family. She answered without hesitation, "I will have no problems. I have bought myself a cook book. I learned to read when I was five."

And I have the cheek to think that I thought up "If you can READ, you can COOK."

TOOLS NEEDED

- *Chopping board or boards.* Ideally keep one for meat and fish and one for vegetables.

- *Knives* – at least 1 large 1 small - sharp enough to cut meat

- *Set of measuring cups.* The standard cup used throughout the book is 220ml (8 fluid ounces). Either buy measuring cups (they are not expensive in supermarkets) or find a plastic container that measures this amount and always use it.

- *Measuring jug* for liquid

- *Scales.* Digital scales that measure in small amounts are very useful. They need not be expensive.

- *Timer.* Useful but not essential

- *Set of measuring spoons* as these will be more accurate than those in the cutlery drawer. In these recipes spoonfuls should be level.

- *Colander* for straining vegetables.

- *Cheese grater*

- *Wooden spoon*

- *Tongs*

- *Potato masher*

- *Oven gloves*

- *Heatproof mats*

- *Big sieve*

- *Garlic press*, if you are going to use fresh garlic.

- *Pastry brush*

- *Tin opener*

- *Potato peeler*

- *Salad spinner.* If you are going to make your own salads.

SOUP

BEAN 'N' SWEETCORN SOUP

🕐 45

Using fresh vegetables? See page 15

Preparation

1. Mix the cornflour with the water.

2. If you are using any fresh vegetables, prepare them now. Peel the potato and chop it on a board into small dice.

3. Drain the beans in a sieve and rinse.

4. Put a large saucepan onto medium heat and add the oil. Add the onions and fry until softened.

5. Add the water+cornflour, milk, sweetcorn, butter beans, parsley, dried mixed herbs, carrots and potato to the saucepan and add the stock cube, broken up. Stir well.

6. Bring to the boil, then turn down the heat and simmer gently, with a lid on the pan, stirring occasionally, for about 20 minutes.

7. Check the seasoning and serve.

Ingredients

1 cup carrots, frozen or fresh, diced

1 cup onions, fresh or frozen, sliced or chopped

1 large fresh potato

1 tablespoon oil

vegetable stock cube

1 cup frozen sweetcorn

1/2 teaspoon dried mixed herbs

1 teaspoon dried parsley

2 tablespoons cornflour

1 large tin butter beans

1 cup water

2 cups milk

salt, pepper

Also try this!

Put grated cheese, croutons or chopped crispy bacon on top.

Add 1 tablespoon curry paste.

CARROT AND TOMATO SOUP

Using fresh vegetables? See page 15

Preparation

1. If you are using using fresh basil and parsley, wash and chop, either onto a board or with kitchen scissors.

2. If you are using any fresh vegetables, prepare them now.

3. Mix the cornflour with the water.

4. Put the oil in large saucepan on medium heat and add the onions and cook until they are soft.

5. Add the carrots, tomatoes, basil, parsley, the stock cube, broken up, and the water+cornflour. Mix well.

6. Bring to the boil, then reduce the heat and cook bubbling slowly, with a lid on the pan, for 20 minutes, stirring occasionally.

7. When it is finished, check the seasoning.

8. Add the crème fraiche.

9. Then, with a potato masher break up the vegetables a bit. Or if you have a food processor, cool the soup and whizz it in a food processor.

Ingredients

2 cups onions, frozen or fresh, sliced or diced

3 cups frozen carrots

large tin chopped tomatoes

vegetable stock cube

2 cups water

2 tablespoons cornflour

2 tablespoons oil

4 tablespoons crème fraiche or low fat crème fraiche

basil: 1teaspoon dried, fresh chopped or frozen

parsley: 1teaspoon dried, fresh chopped or frozen

salt, pepper

Also try this!

Add 1 tablespoon curry paste.

CARROT AND CORIANDER SOUP

🕐 30

*Using fresh
vegetables?
See page 15*

Preparation

1. If you are using fresh coriander or parsley, wash and chop it, either on a board or with kitchen scissors.

2. If you are using any fresh vegetables, prepare them now.

3. Put the oil, onions, garlic, dried coriander and carrots in a large saucepan on moderate heat and stir until the onion is softened.

4. Add the water and the stock cube, broken up.

5. Add the parsley.

6. Check the seasoning.

7. Bring to the boil. Then turn down the heat and put a lid on the pan and cook bubbling gently, stirring occasionally, for 20 minutes.

8. Either mash with a potato masher to break up the carrots or cool the soup and whizz it in a food processor.

9. Add the chopped leaf coriander. See the soup is hot and serve.

Ingredients

2 cups onions, fresh or frozen, sliced or diced

6 cups frozen sliced carrots

garlic: 2 cloves fresh, peeled and crushed, or 1 teaspoon in oil or frozen

1 teaspoon dried ground coriander

parsley: 2 teaspoons dried or 2 teaspoons chopped frozen or fresh

coriander: 2 tablespoons chopped fresh or chopped frozen

vegetable or chicken stock cube

3 cups water

2 tablespoons oil

salt, pepper

Also try this!

Add 1 tablespoon curry paste.

Put a tablespoon of plain yoghurt or fromage frais on the top of each bowl.

ONION SOUP
with cheese
maxi-croutons

Using fresh vegetables? See page 15

Preparation

1. Mix the cornflour into the water.

2. If you are using any fresh vegetables, prepare them now.

3. Put the butter, margarine or oil in a large saucepan on medium heat and add the onions.

4. Gently fry the onions for ten minutes until soft but not browned.

5. Add the milk, broken up stock cube and the nutmeg and pepper. Stir well.

6. Bring to the boil, stirring.

7. Then turn the heat down and cook, bubbling very gently, with a lid on the pan, stirring occasionally, for 30 minutes.

8. When the soup is cooked, add the cornflour+water mixture to the soup and bring it to the boil to thicken.

9. Check the seasoning.

10. While the soup is cooking, make the MAXI-CROUTONS (opposite).

11. When the soup is ready, serve by placing a crouton in the middle of each bowl of soup.

Ingredients

6 cups onions, frozen or fresh, sliced or diced

600 ml (1 pint) milk

50g (2 oz) butter or margarine or 4 tablespoons oil

$1/2$ teaspoon nutmeg

vegetable stock cube

1 tablespoon cornflour

1 cup water

black pepper

4 half-slices regular thick bread, or 4 slices ciabatta or French loaf

approx 50g (2 oz) thinly sliced cheese

MAXI-CROUTONS

Turn the grill on and toast both sides of the bread.

Place the sliced cheese on one side of the toast and grill until browned.

Also try this!

Add a tin of white beans, butter beans or haricot beans, drained and rinsed, at the same time as the cornflour+water, to make a light meal.

MARGARET'S
very substantial
SUPER SOUP

*Using fresh
vegetables?
See page 15*

Preparation

1. Mix the cornflour into the water.

2. If you are using any fresh vegetables, prepare them now.

3. Put the lentils into a sieve and rinse very thoroughly under cold running water.

4. Peel the potatoes and carrots (if using fresh) and sweet potato and cut them into small dice.

5. Put the oil in a large saucepan on medium heat and add the onions. Fry the onions until they are well softened.

6. Add the curry paste and stir well.

7. Add the water+cornflour and stir thoroughly. Add the stock cube, broken up.

8. Add the potatoes, sweet potato, carrots, tomatoes, tomato puree, lentils and bay leaf. Stir well.

9. Bring to the boil. Next, turn down the heat and cook, bubbling very gently, with a lid on the pan, for about 30–40 minutes, stirring occasionally.

10. Check the seasoning and serve.

Ingredients

2 cups onions, frozen or fresh, sliced or diced

2 cups frozen or fresh carrots

1 fresh potato

1 small sweet potato

large tin chopped tomatoes

2 tablespoons tomato puree

vegetable stock cube

150g (5 oz) red lentils

1 tablespoon curry paste

bay leaf

2 tablespoons oil

1 tablespoon cornflour

salt, pepper

3 cups water

TASTE OF TUSCANY

*Using fresh
vegetables?
See page 15*

Preparation

1. Mix the cornflour into the water.

2. If you are using any fresh vegetables, prepare them now.

3. Peel and dice the potato.

4. Put a large saucepan on medium heat and add the oil and onions and fry until the onion is softened.

5. Then add the water+cornflour, garlic, stock cube, broken up, vegetables, pasta, beans, basil or parsley, tomatoes, pepper and potatoes and mix well.

6. Bring to boil, then turn down the heat and cook, bubbling gently, with a lid on the pan, for 20-25 minutes, stirring occasionally.

7. Check that the vegetables and pasta are cooked. Check the seasoning and serve.

Ingredients

2 cups onions, fresh or frozen, sliced or diced

2 tablespoons oil

large can cannellini or haricot beans

2 cups frozen mixed vegetables (peas and carrots)

1 fresh potato

large tin chopped tomatoes

garlic: 2 cloves fresh, 1 teaspoon garlic in oil or frozen

1 teaspoon dried basil or parsley

vegetable stock cube

1 tablespoon cornflour

25g (1oz) dried pasta pieces

3 cups water

salt, pepper

Also try this!

Put grated cheese, either cheddar or parmesan, on top.

Add 1 cup sweetcorn with vegetables. Top with croutons.

Make double amount and add 1 tablespoon curry paste the next day.

CURRIED LENTIL SOUP

Using fresh vegetables? See page 15

Preparation

1. Mix the cornflour into the water.

2. If you are using any fresh vegetables, prepare them now. The carrots should be diced.

3. Rinse the lentils in a sieve under running cold water.

4. Place the oil in a saucepan on medium heat, add the onion and fry until it is well softened.

5. Add the curry paste and mix well.

6. Add the water+cornflour, stock cube broken up, carrots and lentils. Mix well.

7. Bring to the boil, then turn down heat and cook, with a lid on the pan, bubbling gently, for approximately 20 minutes, stirring occasionally.

8. After 20 minutes, check that the carrots are cooked and the lentils soft and breaking up. If the carrots seem too large for soup, break them up with a potato masher.

9. Check seasoning and serve.

Ingredients

1 cup red lentils

onions: 2 cups frozen or fresh, sliced or diced

carrots, 2 cups frozen or fresh

1 tablespoon oil

1 tablespoon curry paste (any flavour)

1 tablespoon cornflour

4 cups water

1 stock cube

Also try this!

Other vegetables such as peas, or stew vegetables, can be added, or a tin of tomatoes.

QUICK
&
TASTY

POTATO BAKE

Preparation

Preheat oven to 180°C (350°F)

1. If you are using fresh vegetables, prepare them now.

2. Grate the cheese

3. Peel the POTATOES. Chop them into quarters.

4. Place them in a saucepan with cold water just to cover. Add $^1/_2$ teaspoon salt. Bring them to the boil and then turn down the heat and cook, gently bubbling, with a lid on the saucepan, until soft, about 15-20 minutes.

5. When the potatoes are cooked, drain in a colander placed in the sink.

6. Return the potatoes to the saucepan and mash firmly, with a potato masher, until there are no lumps left.

7. Then add half the butter or margarine and enough milk to make a fairly soft mixture. Mix with a wooden spoon to make it smooth.

8. While the potatoes are cooking, prepare the onions.

9. Put a frying pan on medium heat

Ingredients

900 g (2 lb) fresh potatoes

3 cups onions frozen or fresh, sliced or chopped

garlic: either 2 cloves fresh, peeled and pressed or 1 teaspoon garlic in oil or frozen

50g (2 oz) butter or margarine

225g (8 oz) cheese, Cheddar type

milk

salt, pepper

4 cups frozen peas or other vegetables, frozen or fresh

safety!

Use oven gloves
Have heatproof mat ready
for finished bake.

with half the butter or margarine and fry the onions until soft and starting to brown a little. Switch off the heat and pull the pan to one side.

10. Add the garlic, onions and cheese to the mashed potato and stir well.

11. Check the seasoning. It will probably need pepper.

12. Place in a greased oven proof dish and cook in the oven for approximately 30 minutes until browned.

13. <u>When the bake has been in the oven for 20 minutes</u> cook the VEGETABLES.

14. Place the peas or other vegetables in a saucepan with a cup of water and a pinch of salt. Bring to the boil and cook bubbling gently, covered, for about 5-10 minutes until just tender when tested with the point of a knife. Drain by using a colander placed in the sink

15. Serve.

Also try this!

Wash cherry tomatoes and bake in oven while the Potato Bake is cooking

Great with bacon or sausages.

Add chopped cooked ham before baking.

POTATOES WITH CHEESE

Using fresh vegetables? See page 15

Preparation

1. If you are using fresh vegetables, prepare them now.

2. Peel the potatoes. Cut into fairly thick slices and place in a pan. Just cover with cold water. Add $1/2$ teaspoon of salt.

3. Bring to the boil. Then reduce the heat, place a lid on the pan and cook, bubbling gently for about 12–15 minutes until cooked but still firm when tested with the point of a knife.

4. Drain over a colander placed in the sink.

5. Next fry the onions in a large frying pan with the oil or oil and butter or margarine until softened.

6. When the onions are beginning to brown, add the potatoes to the pan.

7. Fry until the potatoes are lightly browned.

8. Cut the cheese in small chunks. Add to the pan and stir until it is melted.

9. Season with pepper. Serve.

Ingredients

1.25 kilos (2½ lbs) fresh potatoes (more or less potatoes according to appetite)

175g (6 oz) cheese (Cheddar or Stilton is good)

4 cups onions, frozen or fresh, sliced or diced

4 tablespoons oil or oil and butter or margarine mixed

salt, pepper

salad, to serve

Also try this!

Add a teaspoon of garlic when frying potatoes.

FILLED JACKET POTATOES

 90

*Using fresh
onions?
See page 15*

Cooking the potatoes is the same for each filling. Check the potatoes for dirt, cut out any large blemishes and wash them in cold water. Prick several times with a fork. Place in an oven preheated to 200°C (400°F) and cook for between 1 hour (for an average baking potato) to $1^1/_2$ hours (for a real whopper). Test by poking a knife point in the potato. If it is tender it is cooked. Each filling is for four potatoes.

Ideally start making the filling about 30 minutes before you expect the potatoes to be cooked. If this isn't convenient, make the filling as soon as you have placed the potatoes in the oven and heat up again when serving.

Serve with a salad.

CHEESE AND ONION TOPPING

Preparation

1. If you are using fresh onions prepare them now.

2. Place the oil in a frying pan and put onto medium heat.

3. Fry the onions until they are softened and starting to brown.

4. Remove pan from the heat .

5. Grate the cheese and add it to the onion, stirring well.

6. Cut the potatoes in half and divide the cheese topping among them.

Ingredients

2 cups onions, fresh
or frozen, diced
1 tablespoon oil
175g (6oz) cheese

Also try this!

Fresh tomato, washed and sliced, peppers or washed sliced mushrooms, can be added at the same time as the onions.

**FILLED
JACKET
POTATOES**

*Using fresh
onions & garlic?
See page 15*

MEDITERRANEAN VEGETABLE AND BEAN TOPPING

Preparation

1. If you are using fresh onions and garlic, prepare them now.

2. Drain and rinse the beans.

3. Put the oil in a frying pan on a medium heat.

4. Add the onions and peppers and fry until softened and starting to brown.

5. Add the garlic, tomatoes, tomato puree, basil, herbs, sugar, $1/4$ teaspoon salt, $1/2$ teaspoon pepper and stir well.

6. Add the beans and cook, bubbling slowly until the mixture begins to thicken a little.

7. Serve on halved potatoes.

Ingredients

2 cups onions, fresh or frozen, sliced or diced

garlic: 2 cloves fresh, peeled and crushed or 1 teaspoon garlic in oil or frozen

large tin chopped tomatoes

2 tablespoons tomato puree

1 cup frozen peppers

large tin kidney beans

1/2 teaspoon dried basil

1/2 teaspoon dried mixed herbs

1 tablespoon oil

1 teaspoon sugar

salt,pepper

Also try this!

Add one or two sliced courgettes, peas, or any other quick cooking vegetables with the onions.

Use chick peas instead of, or in addition to, the kidney beans.

Spice up with chili powder (try $1/2$ teaspoon).

Add 1 tablespoon curry paste at the same time as the tomatoes.

*Using fresh
onions?
See page 15*

SALMON TOPPING

Preparation

1. If you are using fresh onions, prepare them now.

2. Drain the salmon and place in a bowl. Remove or break up any large bones. Mash the salmon.

3. Make up the white sauce by mixing the cornflour into the milk and putting it into a saucepan on a moderate heat and stirring until thickened. Add the butter or margarine and season with plenty of pepper and a little salt if needed. Turn off the heat and pull to one side.

4. Put the oil in a saucepan on a moderate heat and add the onion and peppers. Fry until softened and starting to brown.

5. Add the white sauce and salmon. Stir well and cook until everything is well heated through.

6. Check the seasoning and serve on halved potatoes.

Ingredients

Large tin salmon

570ml (1 pint) milk

3 tablespoons cornflour

**25g (1 oz) butter
or margarine**

**2 cups onion, frozen or
fresh, diced or sliced**

1 tablespoon oil

2 cups frozen peppers

Salt, pepper

Also try this!

*Add 110g (4 oz) grated cheese
with the sauce and salmon.*

FILLED
JACKET
POTATOES

*Using fresh
onions?
See page 15*

TUNA TOPPING

Preparation

1. If you are using fresh onions, prepare them now.

2. Drain the tuna.

3. Make up a white sauce by mixing the cornflour into the milk and putting it into a saucepan on a moderate heat and stirring until thickened. Add the butter or margarine and season with plenty of pepper and a little salt if needed. Turn off the heat and pull the pan to one side.

4. Put the oil into a saucepan on a moderate heat and add the onions, mushrooms and peppers.

5. Fry until softened and beginning to brown.

6. Add the sauce and tuna and stir well.

7. Cook, stirring until well heated through.

8. Check the seasoning and serve on halved potatoes.

Ingredients

2 tins tuna

2 cups onions, fresh or frozen, sliced or diced

2 cups frozen peppers

2 cups frozen mushrooms

1 tablespoon oil

275ml ($^1/_2$ pint) milk

2 tablespoons cornflour

25g (1 oz) butter or margarine

salt pepper

Also try this!

Curried baked beans also make an excellent topping (see the next recipe).

CURRIED BAKED BEANS

Using fresh onions? See page 15

Preparation

1. If you are using fresh coriander, wash and chop it on a board or snip it with scissors.

2. If you are using fresh onions, prepare them now.

3. Place the oil in a saucepan on the stove on medium heat

4. Add the onions and fry until they are softened and slightly browned.

5. Add the curry paste and garlic and stir in well for a few moments.

6. Add the beans and heat through, stirring, with the mixture bubbling for several minutes.

7. When it is hot, serve with bread, with a spoonful of yoghourt and a spoonful of chopped coriander on the top.

Ingredients

2 large tins baked beans

2 tablespoons curry paste

2 cups onions, frozen or fresh, diced

garlic:2 cloves fresh, peeled and crushed, or 1 teaspoon garlic in oil or frozen

1 tablespoon oil

natural yoghourt

chopped fresh coriander to put on top(optional)

Bread, to serve

Also try this!

Add a cup of peppers or a cup of mushrooms when frying the onion.

WELSH RAREBIT

Preparation

1. Wash and slice the tomatoes and set aside.

2. Grate the cheese.

3. Put the milk, cornflour, 25g (1oz) butter or margarine, mustard, $^1/_2$ teaspoon pepper and Worcester sauce into a saucepan. Mix very well.

4. Put the saucepan on to a medium heat and cook, stirring all the time until all the ingredients have melted and the sauce has thickened.

5. Add the grated cheese and continue to cook until it has just melted. (Do not cook any longer than this or the cheese will go stringy).

6. Switch off the ring and pull the sauce to one side.

7. Toast the bread and spread with butter or margarine

8. Check the sauce is hot and place equally on each slice of toast and serve with sliced tomatoes.

Ingredients

570ml(1pint) milk

4 tablespoons cornflour

Butter or margarine: 25g (1oz) for sauce, plus some for putting on toast

1 teaspoon made mustard

225g (8oz) cheese (Cheddar type)

1 teaspoon Worcester sauce (optional)

8 slices of bread

pepper

4 tomatoes, to serve

Also try this!

The tomatoes could be cut up and cooked in the cheese sauce.

SCRAMBLED EGGS PLUS

Using fresh onions?
See page 15

Preparation

1. If you are using fresh onions, prepare them now.

2. Break the eggs into a bowl. Add the milk. Beat until well mixed. Season.

3. Wash the tomatoes and cut into quarters.

4. Place the frying pan on a gentle heat. (If you have a non-stick pan this is ideal.)

5. Put the margarine or butter into the frying pan. Add all vegetables and cook until very soft.

6. Add the eggs, stirring well and cook until almost set. Season.

7. Turn off the heat and pull to one side (otherwise the eggs will continue to cook until hard).

8. Cook the toast, butter it and serve.

Ingredients

1 cup onions, fresh or frozen, diced
1 cup frozen peppers
2 tomatoes
garlic (optional)
2 tablespoons margarine or butter, plus extra for spreading on toast.
4 tablespoons milk
6–8 eggs
8 slices of bread for toast
salt, pepper

CAULIFLOWER CHEESE

Preparation

1. Grate the cheese.

2. Wash the CAULIFLOWER. Cut out the hard central stem. Break the rest into small pieces.

3. Put in a saucepan with 1 cup of cold water and a pinch of salt.

4. Bring to the boil and then reduce the heat and cook, bubbling gently, with a lid on the pan for about 10 minutes until just tender when tested with the point of a knife.

5. Drain using a colander placed in the sink and place the cauliflower in a heatproof dish.

6. As soon as the cauliflower is cooking start the CHEESE sauce.

7. Put the milk, mustard and cornflour into a saucepan and mix well.

8. Put on a moderate heat and stir until thickened. Add the butter and cheese and heat until just melted.

9. Check seasoning. It will probably benefit from pepper.

10. Put the cheese sauce on the cauliflower in the dish and place under a hot grill for a few moments until the cheese has browned a little.

Ingredients

1 cauliflower
275ml (1/2 pint) milk
2 tablespoons cornflour
110g (4 oz) cheese, Cheddar type preferably
25g (1oz) margarine or butter
1 teaspoon made mustard
salt, pepper

Don't cook cheese too long or it goes stringy!

NEW ENGLAND BAKED BEANS
and garlic bread

⏱ 35

*Using fresh onions?
See page 15*

Preparation

1. If you are using fresh onions prepare them now.

2. Heat the oven for the GARLIC BREAD, following the instructions on the packet. Or make your own, see the Ingredients section in the Introduction.

3. Drain the beans in a sieve and rinse.

4. Chop the bacon on a board into pieces about 1".square or cut with kitchen scissors.

5. Put a large saucepan on the stove on medium heat. Add the oil and fry the onions until well softened.

6. Next add the bacon and fry until lightly browned.

7. Add the tomatoes, passata, treacle, Worcester sauce, and beans.

8. Cook gently, stirring occasionally, for about 20 minutes.

9. While the beans are cooking, put the garlic bread in the oven, according to the instructions.

10. When everything is ready, serve.

Ingredients

225g (8oz) smoked bacon

2 tablespoons oil

2 cups onions, frozen or fresh, chopped or sliced

2 tins haricot beans

large tin chopped tomatoes

275m (1/2 pint) passata (sieved tomato pulp)

1 tablespoon black treacle

1 tablespoon Worcester sauce

salt, pepper

garlic bread

safety!
Use oven gloves

FAST LENTILS IN PITTA BREAD

 20

*Using fresh vegetables?
See page 15*

Preparation

1. If you are using fresh vegetables, prepare them now.

2. Drain the lentils in a sieve and rinse them.

3. Put the oil in a saucepan on medium heat and add the onions and garlic and fry until well softened.

4. Add the turmeric, cumin and tomatoes and stir very well.

5. Add the lentils to the tomato mixture. Stir.

6. Cook, with a lid on the pan, bubbling gently for 5–10 minutes.

7. Turn off the heat.

8. Check the seasoning.

9. Then heat the pitta bread according to the packet instructions.

10. Split the pitta breads and divide the lentils between them.

Ingredients

2 cups onions, fresh or frozen, sliced or chopped

garlic: 2 cloves fresh crushed, or 2 teaspoons processed garlic in oil or one teaspoon frozen

1 tablespoon oil

large tin chopped tomatoes

1 teaspoon dried turmeric

$1/_2$ teaspoon cumin

1 large tin lentils

4 pitta breads

salt, pepper

Also try this!

Add chopped salad or cottage cheese to the filled breads.

Use individual naan breads.

RICE

COOKING RICE

METHOD 1 "Chinese Rice". You can pick it up with chopsticks

Preparation

1. Rinse the rice well in a sieve under cold water.

2. Place the rice, salt and water in saucepan with a tightly fitting lid.

3. Stir and bring to the boil.

4. When boiling, turn down the heat to very low, put a lid on the saucepan and cook for approximately 15-20 minutes, when the water should have been absorbed and the rice should be tender.

5. Fluff up with a fork.

Ingredients

225g (8oz) long grain white rice

480ml (16 fl oz) water

$1/_2$ teaspoonful salt

OR

$1^1/_4$ cups long grain white rice

$2^1/_2$ cups water

$1/_2$ teaspoonful salt

METHOD 2 "Indian Rice". Every grain is separate

Preparation

1. Put a large pan $1/_2$ full of water on the stove.

2. Bring to the boil.

3. While this is happening rinse the rice well in a sieve under cold water.

4. When the water is boiling add the

Ingredients

Rice and salt as above.

rice and salt, and boil gently, without a lid on the pan, until the rice is tender – about 15–20 minutes.

5. Strain by using a colander placed in the sink.

MICROWAVE RICE

This comes frozen in individual sachets. It takes about four minutes in the microwave. Follow the instructions on the packet.

FANCY RICE

There are many different kinds of flavoured rice on sale. Just follow the instructions on the packet. They can make an interesting substitute for plain rice, or they can be the basis of a quick meal.

A stock cube can also be dissolved in the cooking water to give flavoured rice.

Eggs and, or, grated cheese or fried bacon make flavoured rice into a very quick and easy meal.

TO POACH EGGS

Place a couple of centimeters or 1 inch of cold water into a frying pan (not too shallow a pan). Bring the water to the boil. You need one or two eggs per person. Break each egg into a cup, one at a time, then slide each egg into the boiling water. When they are set, with no remaining transparent parts, remove with a slotted spoon.

TO SCRAMBLE EGGS

For each person: 1 or 2 eggs and $1/2$ or 1 tablespoon of milk. Break all the eggs into a basin with the milk and beat well. Put a pan (preferably non-stick) onto a medium heat. Add the eggs and milk and 1 tablespoon of butter or margarine and a little salt and pepper. Cook stirring until set and remove from heat immediately or the eggs will go hard.

TO FRY EGGS

Place 2 tablespoons oil, or a little more, into a frying pan on a medium heat. You need 1 or 2 eggs per person. Break each egg into a cup and slide each egg into the hot oil. Cook until set.

FAST NASI GORENG

Using fresh onions & garlic? See page 15

Preparation

1. If you are using fresh onions or garlic, prepare them now.

2. Cook the RICE. See page 44.

3. While it is cooking fry the onions in the oil until softened.

4. Then add the nuts and garlic and stir.

5. Then add the peas and stir again.

6. Cook gently for 5 minutes.

7. When the rice is ready add the nuts and vegetables, mix thoroughly and serve.

Ingredients

225g (8oz) 1¹/₄ cups long grain rice

2 tablespoons oil

75g (3oz) nuts (cashews or peanuts)

2 cups frozen peas

garlic: 2 cloves fresh crushed or 1 teaspoon processed garlic in oil

2 cups onions, fresh or frozen, chopped or sliced

Also try this!

Put a fried egg for each person on the top.

Add crisp fried bacon or sliced ham.

CURRY RICE

*Using fresh
onions?
See page 15*

Preparation

1. If you are using fresh onions, pre-pare them now.

2. Rinse the rice in a strainer under a cold tap.

3. Put the oil in a saucepan. Fry the onions until they are softened. Add the curry paste. Mix well.

4. Add the rice and water to the saucepan. Stir well.

5. Bring to the boil, stir well and then turn down to a very low heat.

6. Put the lid on the pan and cook for 20–25 minutes, by which time the rice should be tender and the water absorbed.

Ingredients

225g, 8oz ,$1^1/_4$ cups
long grain rice

2 cups onions sliced or
chopped, fresh or frozen

1 tablespoon curry paste

2 tablespoons oil

$2^1/_2$ cups water

salt

Also try this!

Add 2 cups sweet corn or tin of beans drained and rinsed to the rice and cook together.

Put cooked eggs on top.

Serve with pitta bread and tomatoes, cucumber or salad.

VEGETABLE RICE

Preparation

1. Place rice and all vegetables in fairly large saucepan with tight fitting lid.

2. Boil the water and dissolve the stock cube in it. Add dried herbs and add to the rice and vegetables

3. Stir well.

4. Bring to the boil and then turn down to a low heat with the lid on for about 20 minutes, by which time the rice should be tender and the water absorbed.

5. When the rice is tender fluff up with fork and serve.

Ingredients

225g, 8oz, 1$\frac{1}{4}$ cups, long grain rice

1 cup frozen peppers

1 cup carrots, frozen

sweet corn: 1 cup frozen or tinned

1 cup frozen peas

1 cup mushrooms, frozen sliced

vegetable stock cube

$\frac{1}{2}$ teaspoon mixed dried herbs

2$\frac{1}{4}$ cups water

Also try this!

Put nuts, cheese or cooked eggs on top.

PASTA

MACARONI CHEESE

This recipe depends on doing two things at the same time: cooking the pasta and making the sauce.

Make the sauce while the water for the pasta is heating and continue cooking the sauce during the time the pasta is cooking.

Combine both to finish the dish.

Preparation

Preheat the oven to 180ºC (350ºF)

1. Wash the tomatoes and cut them in half. Wash the mushrooms and place the mushrooms and tomatoes on a baking tray. Sprinkle them with a little pepper or dried herbs and a small amount of oil.

2. Grate the cheese.

3. Spread the margarine or butter on the bread and cut it into small dice.

4. Put a large pan $^2/_3$ full of water on the stove, add 1 teaspoon of salt and bring it to the boil.

5. When it is boiling, add the PASTA pieces. Reduce the heat and cook, gently bubbling, for about 15 minutes until tender.

6. When the pasta is cooked, drain by using a colander placed in the sink.

Ingredients

350g (12 oz) pasta pieces

570ml (1 pint) milk

4 tablespoons cornflour

225g (8 oz) cheese, grated

butter or margarine for spreading on bread and 25g(1oz) for the cheese sauce

3 slices of bread, spread with butter or margarine and cut into small dice

2 teaspoons fajita, jerk, or Cajun seasoning

4 tomatoes

4 mushrooms

oil, small amount

salt, pepper

*Using fresh
vegetables?
See page 15*

Needs a heat-proof oven dish

Then return the pasta to the pan.

7. <u>While the pasta is cooking</u> make the SAUCE by placing the milk and cornflour into a saucepan and mixing well

8. To the pan add the margarine or butter and heat at a moderate temperature and stir continuously until thickened.

9. Next add the grated cheese, stir only until melted (do not overcook cheese or it goes stringy) and then check the seasoning. It probably needs pepper.

10. Mix the sauce into the pasta and place in an oven proof dish.

11. Mix the spicy seasoning and diced bread and scatter on the top of the macaroni .

12. Cook in the oven for about 30 minutes until heated through and the topping has browned.

13. <u>At the same time as the macaroni cheese goes into the oven,</u> put in the tray of tomatoes and mushrooms.

14. Serve when the macaroni cheese is browned.

safety!

*Use oven gloves.
Have heat proof mat
ready for finished casserole.*

Also try this!

If you do not like either tomatoes or mushrooms, cook 4 cups of frozen peas, towards the end of the time the macaroni is cooking

Add small pieces of fried bacon or ham when mixing the sauce into the pasta

Green salad with avocado would be a good contrast with this (see page 13)

MUSHROOM PASTA
and salad

This recipe depends on doing two things at the same time: cooking the pasta and making the sauce.

Make the sauce while the water for the pasta is heating and continue during the time the pasta is cooking.

Whichever finishes first, just keep it warm and combine both to serve.

Preparation

1. If you are using any fresh vegetables, prepare them now.

2. Prepare the salad by washing the lettuce and shaking or spinning it dry. Wash and cut up other the salad items. Place the salad in a bowl.

3. For the PASTA put a large pan $^2/_3$ full of water and a little salt on moderate heat and bring it to the boil.

4. When it is boiling add the pasta pieces. Reduce the heat and cook uncovered for about 15 minutes until it is tender.

5. Drain by using a colander placed in the sink. Then return the pasta to the pan.

6. While the pasta is cooking start the SAUCE by putting the butter or margarine in a large saucepan on

Ingredients

2 cups onions frozen or fresh, chopped or sliced

8 cups frozen sliced mushrooms or 350g (12oz) fresh mushrooms

garlic: 2 cloves fresh, peeled and crushed, or 1 teaspoon garlic in oil or 1 teaspoon frozen

50g (2 oz) margarine or butter

1 teaspoon dried paprika

1 teaspoon dried parsley

1 teaspoon dried oregano or basil

1 tablespoon tomato puree

142ml (5 oz) crème fraiche or low fat crème fraiche

salt, pepper

350g (12oz) pasta pieces

salad, to serve

*Using fresh
vegetables?
See page 15*

moderate heat, adding the onions and frying until they are softened.

7. Next add the mushrooms and fry until the liquid they make is beginning to reduce. You may have to raise the temperature to do this. Turn the heat down again when the liquid has gone.

8. Then add the paprika, parsley, garlic, tomato puree and basil. Stir well and cook for 2 minutes.

9. Add the crème fraiche. Stir well.

10. Check the seasoning and heat through gently for three minutes, not allowing the mixture to boil. Keep warm until the pasta is also ready.

11. When both pasta and mushrooms are ready, serve.

**TOMATO AND
ORANGE SALAD**
Try this salad with Mushroom Pasta. Prepare the tomatoes and peel and slice the oranges. Serve with a salad dressing made with lemon juice, not vinegar (see page 14).

Also try this!

Add 2 cups frozen peas when adding mushrooms.

PASTA BAKE
and peas

This recipe depends on doing two things at the same time: cooking the pasta and making the sauce.

Make the sauce while the water for the pasta is heating and continue during the time the pasta is cooking.

Combine both to finish the dish.

Preparation

Preheat oven to 180°C (350°F)

1. If you are using any fresh vegetables, prepare them now.

2. If you are using fresh mushrooms, rinse and slice them.

3. To start the pasta fill a large saucepan 2/3 full of cold water and add 1 teaspoon of salt. Bring to the boil.

4. When the water is boiling, add the pasta. Reduce the heat and cook, uncovered, gently bubbling for about 15 minutes until tender.

5. Strain the pasta by using a colander placed in the sink. Return the pasta to the saucepan.

6. While the pasta is cooking start the SAUCE by chopping the bacon into 2.5cm (1") pieces.

7. Put the oil in the frying pan on medium heat and fry the bacon,

Ingredients

350g (12 oz) pasta pieces

2 cups onions, fresh or frozen, chopped or diced

225g (8oz) bacon

1 tablespoon oil

2 cups chopped frozen mushrooms or 110g (4oz) fresh

1 tin chopped tomatoes

2 eggs

175g (6 oz) grated cheese + 50g (2 oz) for topping

1teaspoon dried basil

1 teaspoon dried parsley

4 cups frozen peas or other vegetables, frozen or fresh

salt and pepper

Using fresh vegetables? See page 15

Needs a heat-proof oven dish, 23×23cm

onions and mushrooms until soft.

8. Turn off the heat and pull the frying pan to one side.

9. Beak the eggs into a bowl and beat well.

10. To the frying pan add the tomatoes, basil, parsley, eggs and the larger amount of cheese and mix well.

11. Add the contents of the frying pan to the pasta in the saucepan and mix well.

12. Put into the oven proof dish and scatter the reserved cheese on top.

13. Cook in the oven for approximately 30 minutes until the top is browned.

14. <u>15 minutes before the pasta bake is finished</u>, start cooking the VEGETABLES by placing in a saucepan with 1 cup of cold water and a pinch of salt. Bring to the boil, reduce heat and cook, with a lid on the pan, bubbling slowly, for 5–10 minutes until tender when tested with the point of a knife. Drain by using a colander placed in the sink.

safety!

Have heat proof mat ready for finished bake.

Use oven gloves

Also try this!

Add one cup of frozen peppers at the same time as the tomatoes

SALMON PASTA

This recipe depends on doing two things at the same time: cooking the pasta and making the sauce.

Start the sauce while the water for the pasta is heating and continue cooking the sauce during the time the pasta is cooking.

Whichever finishes first, just keep it warm and combine both to serve.

Preparation

1. If you are using any fresh vegetables, prepare them now.

2. Drain the salmon, remove the large bones and mash the salmon flesh.

3. For the PASTA put a large pan 2/3 full of cold water and a little salt on moderate heat and bring it to the boil.

4. When it is boiling add the pasta pieces. Reduce the heat and cook uncovered, bubbling gently, for about 15 minutes until tender.

5. Drain by using a colander placed in the sink and return the pasta to the pan.

6. While the pasta is cooking start the SAUCE. First make up the white sauce according to the packet instructions.

7. Next fry the onions and peppers in the oil over moderate heat until

Ingredients

Large tin salmon

2 packets white sauce mix

milk or water to make up white sauce

1 cup onions: frozen or fresh, sliced or diced

2 cups frozen peppers

2 cups frozen peas or sweetcorn or both

2 tablespoons oil

salt, pepper

350g (12oz) pasta pieces

20

Using fresh vegetables? See page 15

they are softened.

8. Add the peas, mix well and cook for few minutes.

9. Add the salmon to the white sauce.

10. Add the vegetables to the white sauce and mix all well

11. Heat until cooked through.

12. Serve over the pasta.

WHITE SAUCE

You may want to make a white sauce yourself.

Put 570ml (1 pint) milk, 3 tablespoons cornflour, 1 tablespoon butter or margarine, a good pinch of pepper and a little salt in a saucepan (preferably non-stick). Mix well. Place on a medium heat and stir until thickened. Add a pinch of nutmeg if you wish. Add cheese also if you like.

Also try this!

Green salad with avocado would be a good contrast with this (see page 19)

Mushroom salad would also go well with this. Prepare and slice mushrooms (page 17) and add a salad dressing (page 14) with $1/2$ a clove of fresh garlic pressed and added

ITALIAN BOLOGNAISE

Preparation

1. If you are using any fresh vegetables prepare them now.

2. Grate the cheese.

3. Mix the cornflour into the water.

4. Put the oil in a saucepan on moderate heat and fry the onions until well softened.

5. Add the garlic and herbs and stir well.

6. Add the meat and fry until it changes colour. Break up any lumps with a wooden spoon.

7. Add the tomatoes, tomato puree, a good pinch of pepper, water+cornflour and the stock cube, broken up. Mix well.

8. Cook, bubbling slowly, with a lid on the pan for 30–40 minutes. Stir occasionally.

9. As soon as the meat is cooking, start the SPAGHETTI by $^2/_3$ filling a large saucepan with cold water. Add 1 teaspoon salt and bring to the boil.

10. When it is boiling, add the spaghetti, then reduce the heat and cook, bubbling gently, uncovered, for

Ingredients

450g (1 lb) beef mince

onions: 2 cups fresh or frozen, sliced or diced

garlic: 2 cloves fresh, peeled and crushed or 1 teaspoon garlic in oil or frozen

2 tablespoons oil

1 teaspoon mixed dried herbs, or oregano

1 cup water

2 tablespoons cornflour

large tin chopped tomatoes

3 tablespoons tomato puree

stock cube

salt, pepper

350g (12oz) spaghetti (any kind)

4 cups vegetables, frozen or fresh

cheese, to serve

60

 60

*Using fresh
vegetables?
See page 15*

about 15 minutes, until the spaghetti is tender.

11. Drain by using a colander placed in the sink.

12. <u>While the spaghetti is cooking</u>, cook the VEGETABLES by putting them into a saucepan with 1 cup of cold water and a pinch of salt. Bring to the boil, then reduce the heat and cook, bubbling gently, with a lid on the pan for about 5–10 minutes until just tender when tested with the point of a knife. Drain using a colander placed over the sink.

15. To serve, place the sauce on top of the spaghetti and scatter cheese on top.

safety!

Wash boards and utensils used with raw meat thoroughly in hot water and detergent. Do not use for any other food until this has been done. Wash your hands after handling raw meat.

SPEEDY BOLOGNAISE

Speed things up by using a large jar of Bolognaise sauce instead of cooking the tomato sauce from fresh ingredients.

Fry the onion and add the meat (stages 4 and 6), then add the sauce and follow the recipe from stage 8.

Also try this!

Add 2 cups of carrots with the tomatoes. If using fresh carrots, peel and dice and cook until tender in water, separately, before adding them. Frozen carrots can go straight in.

Add a cup of beans, drained and rinsed.

TUNA AND TOMATO PASTA and salad

This recipe depends on doing two things at the same time: cooking the pasta and making the sauce.

Make the sauce while the water for the pasta is heating and continue cooking the sauce during the time the pasta is cooking.

Whichever finishes first, just keep warm and combine both to serve.

Preparation

1. Drain the tuna.

2. If you are using any fresh vegetables, prepare them now.

3. Prepare the salad by washing the lettuce and shaking or spinning it dry. Wash and cut up the other salad vegetables.

4. Drain and chop the sun dried tomatoes.

5. To cook the PASTA, 2/3 fill a large saucepan with cold water and one teaspoon salt. Bring it to the boil.

6. When the water is boiling, add the pasta. Turn down the heat and cook, uncovered, gently bubbling for about 15 minutes until tender.

7. When the pasta is cooked, drain by using a colander placed in the sink.

8. While the pasta is cooking start the SAUCE by putting the oil into a

Ingredients

1 tablespoon oil

2 cups onions, fresh or frozen, sliced or chopped

garlic: 2 cloves fresh, peeled and crushed, or 1 teaspoon in oil or 1 teaspoon frozen

large tin chopped tomatoes

6 sun-dried tomatoes in oil, drained

2 tablespoons tomato puree

2 cans tuna in oil

2 teaspoons dried parsley or basil

1 teaspoon sugar

350g (12oz) pasta pieces

salt, pepper

salad, to serve

*Using fresh
vegetables?
See page 15*

saucepan on a moderate heat and frying the onions until softened and just beginning to brown.

9. Add the tinned tomatoes and tomato puree and stir well.

10. Add the sun-dried tomatoes, garlic, sugar and parsley or basil.

11. Cook gently for 5 minutes.

12. Add the tuna to the tomato mixture and stir well. Check the seasoning.

13. Heat the tuna and tomato mixture gently until warmed through.

14. When the pasta and sauce are both ready, serve.

MUSHROOM SALAD

A mushroom salad goes well with this.

Prepare and slice the mushrooms (page 17) and add a salad dressing (page 14) with $1/2$ a clove of fresh garlic pressed and added. Place onto washed salad leaves or lettuce, or try...

GREEN SALAD WITH GRAPES AND PECANS

Prepare the green salad and wash the grapes (page 19). Make a salad dressing (page 14). Scatter on some pecan nuts.

Also try this!

*Put grated cheese on top.
Serve with garlic bread.
Serve salad with croutons.*

TRADITIONAL LASAGNE

Preparation

Preheat oven to 180°C (350°F)

1. If you are using any fresh vegetables, prepare them now.

2. Grate the cheese into two piles.

3. To make the MEAT SAUCE put a medium saucepan on the stove on medium heat.

4. Add the oil and fry the onions and mince until the onion softens and the mince changes colour.

5. Add the jar of Bolognaise sauce and one cup of extra water (the lasagne absorbs a lot of liquid).

6. Bring to the boil, then simmer, bubbling gently, with the saucepan lid on for about 30 minutes.

7. As soon as the meat is cooking, start the CHEESE SAUCE by putting the milk in a saucepan on the stove. (If you have a non-stick saucepan it will be easy to clean.) Add the cornflour and mix well.

8. On a moderate heat, stir until thickened. Then add the margarine or butter and the larger amount of cheese. Stir until they are just melted. Then switch off the heat

Ingredients

450g (1lb) beef mince

large jar Bolognaise sauce + 1 cup water

2 cups frozen or fresh, chopped onions

2 tablespoons oil

1 pint milk

3 tablespoons cornflour

25g (1oz) butter or margarine

110g (4 oz) cheese + 50g (2oz) extra (Cheddar type)

approx 275g (10oz) dried lasagne (the amount depends on the size of the dish)

4 cups green vegetables, frozen or fresh

salt, pepper

*Using fresh
vegetables?
See page 15*
                                      Needs an oven-proof dish 22×29cm

___

and pull the pan to one side.

9. <u>When both the sauces are ready,</u> assemble the lasagne.

10. Put half the meat sauce in the bottom of the ovenproof dish.

11. Place a layer of LASAGNE sheets on top to make a neat fit.

12. Next put half the cheese sauce on top of the lasagne.

13. Follow with the next layer of lasagne.

14. Put the remaining meat sauce on top of the lasagne.

15. Follow with the final layer of lasagne.

16. Put the second half of the cheese sauce on top. Spread it evenly and sprinkle on the reserved cheese.

17. Place in the oven for about 30–40 minutes, until the pasta is tender.

18. Ten minutes before the lasagne is ready, put the VEGETABLES and a cup of water in a pan and add a pinch of salt. Bring to the boil, then cook for 5–10 minutes, bubbling gently, with the lid on the pan, until just tender when tested with the point of a knife. Drain by using a colander placed in the sink.

19. Serve.

safety!

Use oven gloves.

Have a heat-proof mat ready when taking cooked lasagne from the oven.

Wash boards and utensils used with raw meat thoroughly in hot water and detergent. Do not use for any other food until this has been done. Wash your hands after handling raw meat.

Also try this!

Add two cups sliced frozen mushrooms, or 110g (4oz) fresh mushrooms, washed and sliced, to the meat sauce.

VEGGIE QUORN PASTA

This recipe depends on doing two things at the same time: cooking the pasta and making the sauce.

Make the sauce while the water for the pasta is heating and continue during the time the pasta is cooking.

Whichever finishes first, just keep it warm and combine both to serve.

Preparation

1. If you are using any fresh vegetables, prepare them now.

2. To cook the PASTA, 2/3 fill large saucepan with cold water and one teaspoon salt. Bring to the boil.

3. When the water is boiling add the pasta. Turn down the heat and cook uncovered, gently bubbling, for about 15 minutes until the pasta is tender.

4. When the pasta is cooked, drain it by using a colander placed in the sink. Replace the pasta in the saucepan.

5. While the pasta is cooking, start the SAUCE by putting the oil into a frying pan and frying the onions on a moderate heat until they have softened and are just starting to brown.

6. Add the Quorn, peas and mush-

Ingredients

175g (6oz) Quorn mince

2 cups frozen peas

2 cups frozen mushrooms

2 cups onions, frozen or fresh, sliced or chopped

2 tablespoons pesto sauce

1 tablespoon pine nuts

5 tablespoons crème fraiche or half fat crème fraiche

2 tablespoons oil

350g (12 oz) pasta pieces

salt, pepper

45

*Using fresh
vegetables?
See page 15*

rooms. Cook for 15 minutes, stirring frequently.

7. Add the crème fraiche, pesto and pine nuts and cook gently for five more minutes, stirring.

8. Check the seasoning.

9. When both the pasta and sauce are ready, serve.

TOMATO SALAD

A tomato salad goes well with this.

Wash and slice tomatoes. Mix $^1/_2$ teaspoon sugar, $^1/_2$ teaspoon basil, fresh chopped (gives the best flavour), frozen or diced, pinch black pepper, $^1/_2$ teaspoon salt, 2 tablespoons olive oil and 1 tablespoon vinegar or lemon juice. Pour the dressing over the sliced tomatoes.

Also try this!

Top with grated cheese, or Parmesan.

The cooked Quorn mince could be used either as the base for a Shepherd's Pie, by putting mashed potato on top, or to fill Tortillas or wraps. Jazz up wraps with low fat Greek yoghurt and guacamole, or pour white or cheese sauce on top and bake at 180ºC (350ºF) for 30 minutes.

ZIPPY CARBONARA

This recipe depends on doing two things at the same time: cooking the pasta and making the sauce.

Make the sauce while the water for the pasta is heating and continue during the time the pasta is cooking.

Combine both to finish.

Preparation

1. If you are using any fresh vegetables, prepare them now.

2. Grate the cheese.

3. To cook the PASTA 2/3 fill large pan with cold water and one teaspoon salt. Bring to the boil.

4. When the water is boiling, add the pasta. Reduce the heat and cook, uncovered, bubbling gently, for about 15 minutes until tender.

5. When pasta is cooked, drain it by using a colander placed in the sink. Replace the pasta in the saucepan.

6. While the pasta is cooking start the SAUCE by first chopping the bacon on a board into 2.5cm (1") pieces.

7. Then put the oil in a frying pan on medium heat and fry the bacon until cooked. Then add the garlic and stir.

Ingredients

225g (8oz) bacon

garlic: 1 clove fresh, peeled and crushed or 1 teaspoon garlic in oil, or one teaspoon frozen

3 eggs

175g (6oz) cheese grated

4 tablespoons milk

350g (12 oz) dried pasta pieces, any type

1 tablespoon oil

salt, pepper

4 cups vegetables, frozen or fresh

*Using fresh
vegetables?
See page 15*

8. Turn off the heat and pull the frying pan to one side.

9. Next start the VEGETABLES. Put them in a saucepan with 1 cup of cold water and a pinch of salt. Bring them to the boil, then turn down the heat and cook, with a lid on the pan, bubbling gently, for approximately 5–10 minutes until just tender. When they are ready, drain by using a colander placed in the sink. Return the vegetables to the pan and pull to the side of the stove until the rest is finished.

10. Next break the eggs into a small bowl and add the milk. Beat together until well mixed.

11. To complete, put the bacon pan back on a moderate heat and add the eggs and cheese and stir until thickening.

Do not overcook as the eggs will continue to thicken in the heat of the pasta.

12. Check the seasoning.

13. Add the egg and cheese mixture to the pasta and stir well.

14. Serve.

Also try this!

Add one cup of mushrooms to the bacon when frying.

VEGETARIAN

RED BEAN PIE

Preparation

Preheat oven to 180°C (350°F)

1. If you are using any fresh vegetables, prepare them now.

2. Mix the cornflour into the water.

3. Drain and rinse the beans.

4. Peel the POTATOES and cut into pieces. 8 for a large potato, four for a medium. Place in a saucepan with cold water just to cover and 1 teaspoon salt. Place on medium heat and bring to the boil. Then turn down the heat and cook, with a lid on the pan, bubbling gently, for 15-20 minutes until tender, when tested with a fork.

5. When the potatoes are cooked, drain using a colander placed in the sink. Return the potatoes to the pan. Next mash them with a potato masher until all lumps have been removed.

6. Add a little butter or margarine and milk and mix with a wooden spoon until smooth. Put a lid on the pan and set on one side until the pie base is ready.

7. As soon as the potatoes are cooking start the RED BEAN PIE base, by

Ingredients

large tin red kidney beans

225g (8oz) Quorn mince

2 cups onions, frozen or fresh, sliced or chopped

4 cups carrots, frozen or fresh.

1 tablespoon oil

2 tablespoons soy sauce

2 tablespoons tomato puree

2 teaspoons dried mixed herbs

2 teaspoons dried parsley

1 tablespoon paprika

2 tablespoons cornflour

1.25 kilos (2$^{1}/_{2}$ lb) fresh potatoes

large tin chopped tomatoes

1 cup water

salt pepper

25g (1oz) butter or margarine

small amount milk

*Using fresh
vegetables?
See page 15*

*Needs a heat-proof
oven dish (23×23cm)*

putting the oil into a saucepan on a medium heat and adding the onions and frying until they are well softened.

8. Add the carrots, beans, soy sauce, paprika, parsley, tomato puree, herbs, Quorn mince, water+corn-flour and tinned tomatoes. Stir very well.

9. Bring to the boil and cook gently bubbling, with a lid on the pan, for 15 minutes, stirring occasionally. Turn off the heat.

10. When both the potato and the bean base are ready, put the bean mixture into the oven proof dish, spoon the potato evenly on top and place in the oven for 30–45 minutes, until browned.

11. When browned, serve.

safety!

Use oven gloves

Have heat resistant mat ready for dish when it comes out of the oven.

MUSHROOM SALAD

A mushroom salad goes well with this.

Prepare and slice the mushrooms (page 17) and add a salad dressing (page 14) with $1/2$ a clove of fresh garlic pressed and added.

Also try this!

2 cups frozen peppers could be added at the same time as the carrots.

$1/2$ teaspoon chili powder could be added with the herbs.

Wash and cut the bases off mushrooms, place on oven tray, drip a very little oil on each, scatter with salt and pepper and bake with pie.

Speed the whole thing up with dried potato if you wish. Follow the instructions on the packet.

VEGETABLE CURRY AND RICE

🕐 45

Using fresh vegetables? See page 15

Preparation

1. If you are using any fresh vegetables, prepare them now.

2. Drain the chickpeas.

3. To start the VEGETABLE CURRY put the oil in large saucepan, add the onions and fry until well softened and just starting to brown.

4. Stir in the curry paste and garlic.

5. Add all the vegetables, tomatoes, parsley, basil, chick peas, water and vegetable stock cube, broken up. Stir.

6. Bring to the boil, then turn the heat down to low and cook, gently bubbling, for 20 minutes, with a lid on the pan, stirring occasionally.

7. <u>As soon as the curry is cooking</u> start the RICE. See p. 44.

8. When the curry is cooked, add the crème fraiche and warm for a few minutes until heated through. Check the seasoning. Cover and pull to one side until the rice is ready.

9. When the rice is ready, serve.

Ingredients

2 cups frozen mixed vegetables

4 cups broccoli, frozen or fresh, chopped small

2 cups frozen green beans

2 cups frozen sliced peppers

2 cups sliced onions, frozen or fresh

garlic: 2 cloves fresh garlic, peeled and crushed or 2 teaspoons garlic in oil or frozen

1 large tin chopped tomatoes

4 tablespoons curry paste

1 teaspoon parsley, fresh chopped, dried or frozen

1 teaspoon basil, fresh chopped, dried or frozen

vegetable stock cube

1 large tin chick peas

4 tablespoons crème fraiche or half fat crème fraiche

$1/_2$ cup water

1 tablespoon oil

salt pepper

225g (8oz) $1^1/_4$ cups long grain rice

Also try this!

Scatter some nuts on top.

Serve with tomato, cucumber or salad.

MOGHUL MEMORIES
with rice

Using fresh vegetables? See page 15

Preparation

1. If you are using any fresh vegetables, prepare them now.

2. Mix the cornflour into the water.

3. Drain and rinse the kidney beans.

4. To start the CURRY put the oil, onions and carrots in a large saucepan on the stove on medium heat and fry until the onions are well softened.

5. Add the curry paste and garlic and mix well.

6. To the saucepan add the water + cornflour and stock cube, broken up, and mix well.

7. Now add the kidney beans, raisins, cashews, chutney, brown sugar, and vegetables and mix well.

8. Bring to boil then turn down heat to low and cook, bubbling gently, stirring occasionally, with a lid on the pan for 20 minutes.

9. Turn off the heat and pull the pan to one side until the rice is finished.

10. <u>As soon as the curry is cooking,</u> start the RICE see p. 44.

11. When the rice is ready, serve.

Ingredients

Large tin kidney beans

3 cups frozen or fresh sliced or diced carrots

3 cups onions, fresh or frozen, sliced or diced

3 cloves garlic, fresh, peeled and crushed or 2 teaspoons garlic in oil or frozen

2 tablespoons curry paste

2 tablespoons cornflour

$1^{1}/_{2}$ cups water

vegetable stock cube

3 tablespoons raisins

3 tablespoons cashew nuts

2 tablespoons mango chutney

2 teaspoons brown sugar

4 cups frozen vegetables (peas, broccoli, cauliflower, or green beans)

2 tablespoons oil

225g (8oz) $1^{1}/_{4}$ cups long grain rice

salt, pepper

Also try this!

Chop cucumber and add to plain yoghourt to serve with curry.

LENTIL STEW AND RICE

Preparation

1. If you are using any fresh vegetables prepare them now.

2. Wash the lentils in a sieve under cold running water.

3. Start the LENTIL STEW by putting the oil in a large saucepan on medium heat and adding the onions and peppers and frying until the onions are softened.

4. Add the tomato puree, yeast extract and water. Stir.

5. Add the lentils to the saucepan. Stir. Do not worry if lentils form bubbles on the surface. Just skim them off.

6. Bring to the boil, then turn down the heat to low.

7. Cook with a lid on the pan, bubbling very gently, for about 25 minutes, stirring occasionally. Turn off the heat when finished and pull pan to one side.

8. As soon as the lentils are simmering, cook the RICE. See p. 44.

9. As soon as the rice is cooking start the VEGETABLES by putting them into a saucepan with 1 cup of cold water and a pinch of salt. Bring to

Ingredients

2 cups frozen peppers

2 cups sliced or chopped onions, frozen or fresh

2 tablespoons tomato puree

2 tablespoons oil

1 teaspoon yeast extract

1 cup red lentils

2 cups water

salt, pepper

225g (8oz) 1$^{1}/_{4}$ cups long grain rice

4 cups vegetables, frozen or fresh

*Using fresh
vegetables?
See page 15*

the boil, turn down the heat and cook, bubbling gently, with a lid on the saucepan for approximately 10 minutes until just tender when tested with the point of a knife.

10. Drain by using colander placed in the sink.

11. When the rice is ready, check the seasoning in the Lentil stew and reheat if not hot enough. Serve.

SALAD

For a salad to accompany this dish, try grating carrots and apple together, and add a few raisins. Use any or a mixture of, mayonnaise, plain yoghurt or salad dressing. For an exotic feel, try adding $1/2$ teaspoon vanilla essence and $1/2$ teaspoon cumin to the dressing. Scatter flaked almonds on the top.

COLESLAW

Wash and very finely slice hard white cabbage. Add a little very finely chopped onion (or chives or spring onion). Make a dressing of a mixture of mayonnaise and yoghurt, or just mayonnaise. All sorts of things can be added to this basic recipe to jazz it up. Try chopped pineapple, fruit or grated carrots.

Also try this!

Flavoured rice would be good with this.

Nuts or cheese could be scattered on top.

Salad would be good with this.

BIG BEAN BOWL

with bread

*Using fresh
vegetables?
See page 15*

Preparation

1. If you are using any fresh vegetables, prepare them now.

2. If you are making your own salad, wash and shake leafy items dry, or use salad spinner. Wash and prepare the tomatoes, cucumber, etc.

3. Drain and rinse the beans.

4. Put the oil in a saucepan on medium heat and add the onions, peppers, mushrooms and garlic and fry until softened.

5. Add the curry paste and stir well.

6. Add the beans, tomatoes and mango chutney and cook gently for about 20 minutes.

7. Check the seasoning and serve.

Ingredients

2 cups frozen sliced peppers

2 cups onions, fresh or frozen, sliced or diced

2 cups frozen sliced mushrooms

garlic: 3 cloves peeled and crushed, or 2 teaspoons garlic in oil or frozen

2 large tins mixed beans

1 large tin chopped tomatoes

2 tablespoons curry paste

2 tablespoons mango chutney

2 tablespoons oil

salt, pepper

bread, to serve

salad, to serve

Also try this!

Put a spoon of yoghurt on top and some washed chopped chives, coriander or spring onions if you have them.

INDIAN INSPIRATION

with rice & vegetables

🕐 40

Using fresh vegetables? See page 15

Preparation

1. If you are using using any fresh vegetables, prepare them now.

2. Drain and rinse the lentils.

3. To start the CURRY put the oil in a saucepan on medium heat and add the onions and fry until softened and just starting to brown.

4. Stir in the curry paste, tomatoes and then the lentils.

5. Cook bubbling gently for 5 minutes. Switch off the heat and pull the pan to one side. Check the seasoning.

6. <u>As soon as the curry is cooking</u> start the RICE. See p. 44.

7. <u>While the rice is cooking</u>, cook the VEGETABLES.

8. Put them into a saucepan. Add a cup of water and a pinch of salt.

9. Bring to the boil, reduce heat, cover and simmer gently for 5–10 minutes until just tender when tested with the point of a knife.

10. Drain by using a colander placed in the sink.

11. When the rice and vegetables are ready, reheat the curry and serve.

Ingredients

2 cups onions, fresh or frozen, diced

2 tablespoons curry paste

Large tin chopped tomatoes

2 tablespoons oil

2 tins lentils

225g (8 oz) 1^1/$_4$ cups rice (flavoured rice is very good with this. See RICE, p. 44

4 cups frozen vegetables or 350g (12oz) fresh broccoli or cauliflower

salt, pepper

Also try this!

Add nuts to the curry.

Serve with relishes, such as chopped tomato, cucumber, or mango chutney.

LENTIL CURRY
with rice, tomato and cucumber

⏱ 60

Using fresh vegetables? See page 15

Preparation

1. Wash the tomatoes and cucumber. Slice and set aside on a dish. Prepare any other fresh vegetables.

2. Rinse lentils in running cold water.

3. Wash the apple, remove the core and chop it, on a board, into pieces.

4. Mix the cornflour into the water and set aside.

5. To start the CURRY, put the oil into a saucepan and place on the stove on medium heat.

6. Add the onions and fry until softened and just starting to brown.

7. Add curry paste and garlic and stir.

8. Add the tinned tomatoes, water + cornflour, apple, bay leaf, sultanas and lentils and mix well.

9. Bring to the boil, reduce the heat and cook, bubbling gently, with a lid on the pan for about 20 minutes until the lentils are soft and the apple cooked. Stir now and again.

11. <u>As soon as the curry is cooking</u>, start the RICE see p. 44.

12. When the rice is ready, check the curry is hot and serve with the tomatoes and cucumber.

Ingredients

1 cup red lentils

2 cups onions: fresh or frozen, diced or sliced

garlic: 2 cloves fresh, peeled and crushed, or 1 teaspoon garlic in oil or frozen

1 eating apple

2 tablespoons oil

2 tablespoons curry paste

2 tablespoons sultanas

1 tablespoon cornflour

large tin tomatoes

3 cups water

1 bay leaf

salt, pepper

225g (8 oz) 1$^{1}/_{4}$ cups long grain rice

4 tomatoes, $^{1}/_{2}$ cucumber, for salad to serve

If the curry is ready before the rice, turn off the heat and pull the curry to one side until the rice is finished.

Also try this!

This is very good served with plain yoghourt and chutney.

BEAN GOULASH
with rice

Using fresh vegetables? See page 15

Preparation

1. If you are using fresh mushrooms, wash them, remove the base of the stalk and chop the rest.

2. Prepare any other fresh vegetables which are being used.

3. Peel the potato and slice thinly.

4. Open the kidney beans, drain and rinse them.

5. To start the GOULASH put the oil in a large pan on medium heat and add the onions and cook until softened.

6. Add the peppers, garlic, mushrooms, paprika, chili, parsley and mixed herbs. Stir well.

7. Add the tin of tomatoes, tomato puree, soy sauce, beans and potato. Stir well until boiling.

8. Reduce heat and cook, with a lid on the pan, bubbling gently, for about 20 minutes, stirring occasionally. Turn off the heat and pull to one side if the goulash is finished before the rice.

9. As soon as the goulash is cooking start the RICE. See p. 44.

10. When the rice is finished, serve.

Ingredients

large tin red kidney beans

2 cups onions, frozen or fresh sliced or diced

2 cups frozen peppers

2 cups frozen sliced mushrooms or fresh equivalent chopped, about 110g (4 oz)

2 tablespoons oil

$1/_2$ teaspoon chili powder (more if you like it hot)

garlic: 3 cloves fresh, peeled and crushed or 2 teaspoons garlic in oil or frozen

1 fresh potato very thinly sliced

1 tablespoon paprika

1 teaspoon mixed dried herbs

1 teaspoon dried parsley

3 tablespoons tomato puree

large tin tomatoes

1 tablespoon soy sauce

225g (8oz) $1^1/_4$ cups long grain rice

salt, pepper

Also try this!

Put a spoonful of plain yoghurt on the top and a scattering of chopped fresh chives or parsley if you have them.

MUSHROOM STROGANOFF
with noodles

Preparation

1. Wash the lettuce and shake or spin dry. Wash and prepare the other salad items.

2. If you are using using celery, prepare by washing. Then remove tough strings and cut the sticks into small pieces.

3. If you are using fresh mushrooms prepare them by rinsing in cold water and picking off any dirt. Cut off and throw away the base of the stalks. Slice up the rest.

4. Prepare any other fresh vegetables which are being used.

5. Mix the water and cornflour.

6. Next start the STROGANOFF by placing the oil in a large frying pan and adding onions and frying until softened.

7. Add the celery or peppers, garlic and mushrooms and fry until the juice made by the mushrooms is reduced a bit. (You will probably have to raise the temperature to do this. Turn heat down again when most of the juice has gone.)

8. Add the water + cornflour mixture, yeast extract and herbs and stir.

Ingredients

2 cups onions, frozen or fresh, chopped or sliced

garlic: 3 cloves fresh, peeled and crushed or 1 teaspoon garlic in oil or frozen

4 sticks celery or 2 cups sliced frozen peppers

8 cups frozen sliced mushrooms or equivalent fresh, about 450g (16oz)

1 tablespoon cornflour

1 cup water

2 tablespoons oil

1 teaspoon yeast extract

I teaspoon mixed herbs

4 tablespoons crème fraiche or reduced fat crème fraiche

salt, pepper

4 blocks noodles (medium egg noodles are best).

Salad to serve

*Using fresh
vegetables?
See page 15*

9. Cook gently for about two minutes.

10. Check the seasoning. You will probably need to add pepper. Turn off the heat and pull the pan to one side while the noodles cook.

11. To cook the NOODLES fill a large saucepan three-quarters full of cold water. Bring the water to the boil and add 1 teaspoon of salt.

12. When the water is boiling, add the noodles and boil for about four minutes, breaking up the blocks of noodle with a fork.

13. When the noodles are tender, drain them by using a colander placed in the sink.

14. Complete the Stroganoff by adding the Crème Fraiche or reduced fat Crème Fraiche, and heating until hot.

15. Serve.

ACCOMPANIMENT

To increase the protein content of this meal, scatter peeled and chopped hard boiled eggs on the top.

Boil the eggs in water for 15 minutes. Drain them and put them immediately into cold water. This prevents a dark line forming round the yolk. Peel off the shells, chop and scatter on top of the stroganoff.

Also try this!

Add 2 cups peas when adding the water to the stroganoff.

COWBOY QUORN CHILI
with rice & vegetables

Preparation

1. If you are using any fresh vegetables prepare them now.

2. Drain and rinse the kidney beans.

3. To start cooking the CHILI put the oil in a large saucepan on moderate heat.

4. Fry the onions for a few minutes until softened.

5. Add the Quorn mince and stir for a few minutes.

6. Add the chili powder, garlic, oregano and cumin, and then stir well.

7. Add the tin of tomatoes, stock cube, broken up, and tomato puree, and then stir well.

8. Add the beans to the saucepan.

9. Cook, gently bubbling, with a lid on the pan, for about 30 minutes, stirring occasionally.

10. <u>As soon as the chili is cooking</u>, start the RICE. See p. 44.

11. <u>While the rice is cooking</u>, start the VEGETABLES.

12. Place the vegetables, fresh or frozen into a saucepan and add one

Ingredients

225g (8oz) Quorn mince

garlic: 2 cloves fresh, peeled and crushed or one teaspoonful garlic in oil or frozen

2 tablespoons oil

1/2 teaspoon chili powder (this will be mild – if you like it stronger, taste before it is totally cooked and add more)

2 teaspoons dried oregano

1 teaspoon ground cumin

Onions, 2 cups fresh or frozen, sliced or diced

1 large tin chopped tomatoes

2 tablespoons tomato puree

vegetable stock cube

large tin kidney beans

salt, pepper

225g (8oz) 1 1/4 cups long grain rice

350g (12 oz) fresh broccoli or 4 cups green vegetables, frozen or fresh

Using fresh
vegetables?
See page 15

cup of cold water and a pinch of salt. Bring to the boil, then turn down the heat and cook gently, with a lid on the saucepan, for about 5–10 minutes, until the vegetables are just tender when tested with the point of a knife.

13. Drain by using a colander placed in the sink.

14. Check chili seasoning, and then serve.

Quorn Chili is very versatile. Try using it as the base for Shepherd's Pie, or for filling tortillas or wraps and baking in the oven, for about 30 minutes at 180ºC (350ºF) with a white sauce or cheese sauce topping.

WHITE SAUCE

Put 275ml ($^1/_2$ pint) of milk, 1 tablespoon cornflour, $^1/_2$ tablespoon butter or margarine in a saucepan (preferably non-stick). Mix well. Place on a medium heat and stir until thickened.   Add seasoning. Add cheese   if wished.

Also try this!

For a salad to accompany this dish try grating carrots and apples together, and adding a few raisins. Use any or all of mayonnaise, plain yoghurt or salad dressing. For an exotic feel, try adding $^1/_2$ teaspoon vanilla essence and $^1/_2$ teaspoon cumin to the dressing. Scatter flaked almonds on the top.

Add two cups of frozen carrots to the chili at the same time as the beans.

Put a spoonful of yoghourt on the top of each serving.

FISH

GRILLED CAJUN SALMON
with fried vegetables

Preparation

1. Line the grill pan with kitchen foil. It will be easier to clean and will not leave it smelling of fish.

2. Wash and slice the tomatoes.

3. If you are using any fresh vegetables prepare them now.

4. Rinse the salmon under cold water.

5. Scatter the Cajun spices evenly on top of the salmon and set aside for a few minutes.

6. Next start POTATOES. Wash them and remove any dirt or blemishes and place in saucepan, just cover with water and add 1/2 teaspoon of salt.

7. Bring to the boil, then reduce the heat and cook, bubbling slowly, with a lid on the pan, for about 15 minutes until they feel tender when pressed with the tip of a knife.

8. Then turn off the heat and drain by using a colander placed in the sink. Return the potatoes to the saucepan and leave them covered until everything is completed.

9. <u>As soon as the potatoes are cooking</u>, start the VEGETABLES by

Ingredients

4 fillets fresh salmon

4 teaspoons Cajun spice

onions: 4 cups diced, either frozen or fresh

4 tomatoes

either 2 cups frozen peppers or 2 cups frozen mushrooms (or both)

2 tablespoons oil + 1 tablespoon for oiling pan

700g (1$^1/_2$ lb) new potatoes

salt, pepper

Using fresh vegetables? See page 15

placing 2 tablespoons of oil in a large frying pan and adding the onions, tomatoes and peppers or mushrooms. Fry gently until they are all softened. Season with salt and pepper. As soon as they are cooked, remove the pan from the heat and leave on one side.

10. <u>As soon as the vegetables are cooking</u> preheat the grill to moderately hot.

11. Spread a little oil on the foil lined pan. Place the SALMON pieces in the pan in a single layer.

12. Place under the grill for 8-10 minutes.

13. Then test to see if it is cooked. The length of time the fish takes will depend on its thickness and the heat of the grill. To check if it is cooked through, gently prise apart the flakes with a knife point. There should be no redness left in the centre. If there is redness, give it a little longer. Try not to over cook fish.

14. Serve by piling the vegetables equally onto four plates and putting a piece of salmon on the top of each.

safety!

Remove any fish bones

This recipe also works well using trout fillets, but the cooking time should be shortened as they are usually thinner than salmon.

Also try this!

Serve with a salad or an extra vegetable.

Add 2 cups of frozen peas to the vegetables when they are frying.

Add garlic when frying the vegetables.

CHINESE SALMON
with rice & vegetables

Preparation

1. Line the grill pan with foil. It will be easy to clean and will not leave it smelling of fish.

2. Mix the Chinese five spice, brown sugar, garlic, ginger and soy sauce in bowl.

3. If you are using any fresh vegetables prepare them now.

4. Start the RICE. See p. 44.

5. Rinse the salmon in cold water and set aside for a few minutes.

6. As soon as the rice is cooking start the VEGETABLES by placing them in a saucepan with 1 cup of cold water and a pinch of salt.

7. Bring to the boil, then turn down the heat and cook, covered, bubbling gently for 5-10 minutes until tender.

8. When tender, drain by using a colander placed in the sink.

9. If vegetables are finished before the fish or the rice, drain the vegetables, return them to the pan and pull the pan to one side, covered, until the fish or rice is ready.

10. As soon as the vegetables are cook-

Ingredients

4 fillets of fresh salmon

1 teaspoon Chinese 5 spice powder

1 teaspoon brown sugar

ginger:1 teaspoon fresh grated or ginger in oil

garlic: 2 cloves fresh, peeled and crushed or one teaspoon garlic in oil or frozen

3 tablespoons soy sauce

1 tablespoon of oil for greasing pan.

225g (8oz) 1$\frac{1}{4}$ cups long grain rice

4 cups green vegetables, frozen or fresh, cut small.

Using fresh vegetables? See page 15

___

ing start the FISH.

11. Preheat the grill to a fairly high heat.

12. Oil the foil in the grill pan and place the fish in a single layer in the pan.

13. Spoon or brush the sauce on top and cook it under a fairly high temperature for about 8 minutes.

14. The length of time the fish takes will depend on its thickness. To check if it is cooked through, gently prise apart the flakes with the point of a knife. There should be no redness left in the centre. If there is redness, give it a little longer. Try not to over cook fish.

15. When everything is ready, serve.

safety!

Remove any fish bones

This recipe also works well using trout fillets, but the cooking time should be shortened as they are usually thinner than salmon.

Also try this!

The topping works wonderfully well on chicken pieces, cooked in the Quick Chick way. If you are using fresh garlic and ginger, add a tablespoon of oil, otherwise there will be enough oil in the processed garlic or ginger.

PRAWN CURRY

with rice & vegetables

Preparation

1. Defrost the prawns by taking them out of their bag and placing them in cold water until unfrozen. Drain thoroughly when thawed.

2. If you are using any fresh vegetables prepare them now.

3. Wash and chop the fresh coriander, either on a board or with kitchen scissors.

4. To start the CURRY SAUCE put the oil in a saucepan and place on moderate heat.

5. Add the onions and fry until they are softened and beginning to brown.

6. Add the garlic, ginger, a good pinch of pepper and the curry paste and stir well.

7. Add the tomatoes.

8. Cook, bubbling slowly, for 15 minutes until it is a little thicker and reduced in quantity.

9. Turn off the heat and pull the pan to one side for a few moments.

10. As soon as the curry sauce is cooking, start the RICE. See p. 44.

11. Next start the VEGETABLES by

Ingredients

350g(12oz) frozen prawns

onions: 2 cups diced, frozen or fresh

garlic: 2 cloves fresh, peeled and crushed or 1 teaspoon garlic in oil or frozen

ginger: 1 teaspoon fresh chopped or 1 teaspoon ginger in oil

1 tablespoon oil

1 tablespoon curry paste

1 large tin chopped tomatoes

2 tablespoons fresh or frozen coriander or 2 teaspoons freeze dried

225g (8 oz) 1$^1/_4$ cups long grain rice

4 cups frozen green beans or other green vegetable, frozen or fresh

salt, pepper

*Using fresh
vegetables?
See page 15*

*Allow defrosting time for the
prawns: check the packet carefully!*

placing in saucepan with 1 cup of water and a pinch of salt.

12. Bring to the boil and cook, bubbling gently, covered for about 5-10 minutes until tender when tested with the point of a knife.

13. Drain by using a colander placed in the sink.

14. As soon as the vegetables are cooking it is time to finish the prawn curry by checking the prawns are well drained and placing them into the curry sauce.

15. Bring the sauce to the boil, then turn down the heat and cook, bubbling very gently, for about 3-5 minutes until the prawns are heated right through.

16. Add the coriander and serve.

Also try this!

Make this into fish stew by substituting fillets of white fish or salmon, cut into cubes, for the prawns. Allow a few more minutes for stage 15 but do not overcook.

Experiment with adding other seafood.

HOT PEPPERED FISH

with mashed potatoes

Preparation

1. Line the grill pan with kitchen foil. It will be easy to clean and will not leave it smelling of fish.

2. If you are using any fresh vegetables prepare them now.

3. Wash and chop the fresh coriander, either onto a board or with kitchen scissors.

4. To make the topping, mix the coriander, black pepper, chili pepper, dried parsley, salt, garlic and 2 tablespoons of oil in a bowl.

5. Rinse the fish in cold water.

6. Spread the topping on the fish.

7. Peel the POTATOES and chop into pieces approximately 2.5cm (1").

8. Put the potatoes into a saucepan and just cover with water. Add 1 teaspoon salt.

9. Bring to the boil and cook, bubbling gently, with a lid on the pan, for 15-20 minutes until tender.

10. Turn off the heat and drain the potatoes by using a colander placed in the sink.

11. Return the potatoes to the pan and mash, with a potato masher, press-

Ingredients

4 fillets fresh white fish, cod, haddock or similar

1 tablespoon fresh or frozen coriander or 2 teaspoons freeze dried

1 teaspoon black pepper

$1/4$ teaspoon chili pepper

2 teaspoons dried parsley

$1/2$ teaspoon salt

garlic: 2 cloves, peeled and crushed or 1 teaspoon garlic in oil or frozen

2 tablespoons oil for fish topping and 1 tablespoon oil for greasing pan

4 cups green vegetables, frozen or fresh

900g (2 lb) fresh potatoes

*Using fresh
vegetables?
See page 15*

ing downwards firmly until all lumps are removed. Leave in the saucepan, covered, until everything else is ready.

12. <u>As soon as potatoes are cooking</u> start the VEGETABLES by placing them in a saucepan with 1 cup of cold water and a pinch of salt.

13. Bring to the boil, turn down the heat and cook, covered, bubbling gently for 5–10 minutes until tender when tested with the point of a knife.

14. Drain by using a colander placed in the sink. Return them to the saucepan. Leave it covered, until everything else is ready.

15. <u>As soon as the vegetables are cooking</u>, preheat the grill to a fairly high temperature.

16. Start to cook the FISH by oiling the foil lined grill pan.

17. Place the fish pieces on it in a single layer.

18. Grill under a fairly hot heat for approximately 8 minutes.

19. The length of time the fish takes will depend on its thickness.

20. When everything is ready, serve.

safety!

Remove any fish bones you find

To check if the fish is cooked through, gently prise apart the flakes with a knife point. It should be white all through. If it is not, give it a little longer. Try not to overcook fish.

Also try this!

Cream the potato by adding a little butter and margarine and a little milk and mixing with a wooden spoon until smooth.

Add fresh, chopped or dried herbs to Greek yoghourt or mayonnaise. Add a dollop when serving.

Fry onion, garlic, tomatoes and peppers until soft and serve the fish on top of this.

MEDITERRANEAN BAKED FISH

Preparation

Preheat the oven to 180°C (350°F)

1. If you are using any fresh vegetables, prepare them now.

2. Rinse the fish in cold water.

3. Wash and slice the tomatoes.

4. Wash the potatoes and place in a saucepan with 1 teaspoon salt. Just cover with water. Leave aside for a short while.

5. Place the oil in a frying pan on a medium heat and fry the onions until they are softened and beginning to brown.

6. Then place the fried onions in the bottom of the baking dish and set the FISH on top of them.

7. Arrange the sliced tomatoes on top of the fish and scatter the parsley and basil evenly on top. Season with salt and black pepper.

8. Put in the oven for 15–20 minutes.

9. It should be done after this time but the length of time the fish takes will depend on its thickness.

10. <u>As soon as the fish is in the oven</u> put the POTATOES onto a medium heat, bring to the boil and then

Ingredients

4 fillets fresh cod or other fresh white fish

4 tomatoes

onions: 2 cups diced, fresh or frozen

2 tablespoons oil

1 teaspoon dried basil

1 teaspoon dried parsley

700g (1$\frac{1}{2}$ lb) new potatoes

4 cups frozen green beans or other fresh or frozen vegetables

salt, pepper

To check if it is cooked through, gently prise apart the flakes with the point of a knife. If the fish is white all through it is done. Do not over cook fish.

⏰ 40

*Using fresh
vegetables?
See page 15*

*Needs a metal
baking dish*

reduce the heat and cook, covered, bubbling gently, for about 15 minutes, until they are tender, when tested with the point of a knife.

11. Turn off the heat. Drain them by using a colander placed in the sink and return to saucepan. Cover until the rest of the meal is completed.

12. <u>As soon as the potatoes are cooking</u>, cook the VEGETABLES. Place them in a saucepan with 1 cup of water and a pinch of salt. Bring to the boil, then turn down the heat and cook, bubbling gently, with a lid on the pan for approximately 10 minutes until tender. Drain by using a colander placed in the sink.

13. When everything is ready serve.

safety!

Use oven gloves

Have heat proof mat ready for dish when it come out of the oven.

Remove any fish bones you find.

Also try this!

Oven baking can be used for any of the grilled fish recipes in this section. Just lightly oil a metal baking dish and follow the baking instructions given here when you have put the topping on the fish.

MEAT

BEEF AND ORANGE CASSEROLE

Preparation

Preheat oven to 180°C (350°F)

1. If you are using any fresh vegetables, prepare them now.

2. If you are not using pre-cut meat, rinse the beef in cold water. On a board, cut off any fat and then cut the rest into cubes.

3. Wash the oranges very well and grate off the peel with a fine grater. Keep the grated peel.

4. Cut the oranges in half and squeeze the juice from the oranges by either using an orange squeezer or by squeezing hard with your hands. Make the juice up to 2 cups with commercial orange or apple juice.

5. Mix the cornflour into the orange juice.

6. Check the POTATOES for dirt. Cut out any large blemishes and wash them in cold water.

7. Now start the CASSEROLE by putting the oil in a frying pan on medium heat, adding the onions and cooking until the onions are softened.

8. Add the beef and stir until it

Ingredients

700g (1$^1/_2$ lbs) stewing steak preferably pre-cut into cubes

2 cups onions, frozen or fresh sliced or diced

2 cups carrots, either frozen or fresh, diced

2 oranges (These will be used for both grated peel and juice.)

2 cups orange juice (Use the juice from the oranges made up with orange juice, or apple juice.)

2 tablespoons tomato puree

2 tablespoons oil

2 tablespoons soy sauce

$^1/_2$ teaspoon chili powder

1 tablespoon cornflour

vegetables: either fresh broccoli, about 350g (12oz) or 4 cups frozen or fresh vegetables

salt, pepper

4 baking potatoes

changes colour.

9. Add the chili powder and tomato puree and stir very well.

10. Put the contents of the frying pan into the casserole.

11. Add the orange juice+cornflour, soy, carrots and orange rind and stir very well.

12. Into the oven, place the casserole, with the lid on and <u>at the same time</u>, the potatoes. Cook for $1\frac{1}{2}$ hours.

13. <u>When the casserole has been cooking for</u> $1\frac{1}{4}$ hours, cook the VEGETABLES by placing them in a saucepan with 1 cup of cold water and a pinch of salt. Bring to the boil, then reduce the heat and cook, with a lid on the pan, gently bubbling for 5-10 minutes until just tender when tested with the point of a knife. Drain by using a colander placed in the sink.

14. <u>After the casserole has been in the oven</u> for $1\frac{1}{2}$ hours check meat and potatoes are cooked and serve.

Safety!

Use oven gloves.

Have a heatproof mat ready for finished casserole.

Wash boards and all utensils used with raw meat very thoroughly in detergent and hot water and do not use with anything else until this has been done. Wash your hands after handling raw meat.

Also try this!

Although I think that casseroling meat in the oven gives a better result, this recipe can be cooked on top of the cooker in a saucepan.

Omit pre-heating the oven and follow the instructions to stage 9, using a large saucepan, not a frying pan. Add the rest of the contents (stage 11). Cook, bubbling gently, for $1\frac{1}{2}$ hours, with a lid on the saucepan, stirring occasionally. Serve with new boiled or mashed potatoes and vegetables.

BEEF AND TOMATO CASSEROLE

Preparation

Preheat oven to 180°C (350°F)

1. If you are using any fresh vegetables prepare them now.

2. Mix the cornflour into the water.

3. Check the potatoes for dirt, remove any large blemishes and wash them in cold water.

4. If you are not using pre-cut beef, rinse the beef and cut on a board into cubes.

5. Put the oil in a saucepan on moderate heat, add the onions and garlic and fry until well softened.

6. Add the BEEF and carrots and fry until the beef changes colour.

7. Put the beef into the casserole.

8. Then, into the casserole, put the tomato puree, a good pinch of pepper, paprika, mixed herbs, parsley, bay leaves, tinned tomatoes, stock cube broken up and the cornflour+water. Stir very thoroughly.

9. Put a lid on the casserole and place the casserole in the oven for 1½ hours. At the same time, place the potatoes in the oven.

10. After the casserole and potatoes

Ingredients

700g (1½ lbs) stewing beef, preferably pre-cut into cubes

2 cups carrots, frozen or fresh, sliced or diced

2 cups onions, fresh or frozen, sliced or diced

garlic: 2 cloves fresh, peeled and crushed or 1 teaspoon processed in oil or frozen

large tin chopped tomatoes

2 tablespoons tomato puree or sundried tomato puree

2 tablespoons oil

2 tablespoons paprika

2 bay leaves

1 teaspoon mixed dried herbs

1 teaspoon dried parsley

½ cup water

1½ beef stock cubes

1 tablespoon cornflour

salt, pepper

4 baking potatoes

4 cups vegetables, frozen or fresh

Using fresh vegetables? See page 15

Needs a heat-proof oven casserole dish with lid

have been in the oven for $1^1/_4$ hours cook the VEGETABLES.

11. Place the vegetables in a saucepan with 1 cup water and a pinch of salt. Bring to the boil, then turn down the heat and cook, with a lid on the saucepan, bubbling gently for approximately 5–10 minutes, until tender when tested with the point of a knife. Drain by using a colander placed in the sink.

12. When everything is ready, serve.

safety!

Use oven gloves

Have heat-proof mat ready for finished casserole

Wash boards and all utensils used with raw meat very thoroughly in detergent and hot water and do not use with anything else until this has been done. Wash your hands after handling raw meat.

Also try this!

Add a tin of drained rinsed beans when assembling the casserole.

Although I think that casseroling meat in the oven gives a better result, this recipe can be cooked on top of the cooker in a saucepan.

Omit pre-heating the oven and follow the instructions to stage 6, then add the other ingredients to the saucepan. Cook, bubbling gently, for $1^1/_2$ hours, with a lid on the saucepan, stirring occasionally.

If you want to spice it up, add a tablespoon or two of curry paste or $^1/_2$ teaspoon of chili powder. If you want to feed your friends too, add a drained and rinsed tin of kidney beans. Serve with mashed potatoes or rice.

SPICY BEEF HOTPOT
with jacket potatoes

Preparation

Preheat oven to 180°C (350°F)

1. If the beef is not pre-cut, rinse under the cold tap and cut on a board into cubes of approximately 2.5cm (1").

2. If you are using any fresh vegetables, prepare them now.

3. Check the POTATOES for dirt. Cut out any large blemishes and wash in cold water.

4. Drain and rinse the beans.

5. Mix the cornflour into a little cold water.

6. To start the BEEF HOTPOT place the oil in a saucepan on medium heat and add the onions and fry until they are softened. Add the beef.

7. Fry, stirring, until the beef has changed colour.

8. Add the carrots, cumin, coriander, garlic, chili powder, a good pinch of pepper and mixed herbs and stir very well.

9. Add the beans to the pan, along with tomatoes, water+cornflour and stock cubes broken up.

Ingredients

700g(1$^1/_2$ lbs) stewing beef, preferably pre-cut into cubes

2 cups onions, fresh or frozen, diced or sliced

2 cloves fresh garlic, peeled and crushed, or 1 teaspoon processed garlic in oil or frozen

2 cups carrots, frozen or fresh

1 teaspoon dried cumin

2 teaspoons dried coriander

I large tin kidney beans

$^1/_2$ teaspoon chili powder

2 teaspoons dried mixed herbs

1 large tin chopped tomatoes

1$^1/_2$ beef stock cubes

1 tablespoon cornflour

2 tablespoons oil

salt, pepper

4 baking potatoes

4 cups green vegetables, fresh or frozen

*Using fresh
vegetables?
See page 15*

Needs a heat-proof oven casserole dish with lid

---

10. Bring to the boil and transfer to the casserole. Put the lid on the casserole.

11. Put the casserole in the oven for 1½ hours. <u>At the same time also place the potatoes in the oven</u>.

12. After the casserole has been cooking for 1¼ hours start the VEGETABLES.

13. Put the vegetables and one cup of cold water and a little salt in a saucepan, bring to the boil.

14. Turn down the heat and cook for approximately 5–10 minutes, until just tender when tested with the point of a knife.

15. Check everything is cooked and serve.

Safety!

Use oven gloves.

Have heatproof mat ready for finished casserole.

Wash boards and all utensils used for raw meat well in detergent and hot water and do not use for anything else until this is done. Wash your hands after handling raw meat.

Also try this!

Bake halved tomatoes for half an hour in the oven instead of the vegetables.

Although I think that casseroling meat in the oven gives a better result, this recipe can be cooked on top of the cooker in a saucepan.

Omit pre-heating the oven and follow the instructions to stage 9. Stir. Cook, bubbling gently, for 1½ hours, with a lid on the saucepan, stirring occasionally.

SLOW-COOKED BEEF CASSEROLE

Preparation

Preheat the oven to 160°C (320°F)

1. Mix the cornflour into the water.

2. Rinse the beef. Cut downwards onto a board. Remove any large bits of fat and cut the beef into large pieces or portion sized pieces.

3. Prepare the onions and root vegetables (except the potatoes). Cut the root vegetables into fairly large pieces.

4. The potatoes and green vegetables will be prepared later.

5. Put the root VEGETABLES (except the onions) into the casserole.

6. Place the oil in the frying pan and fry the onions until they are softened. Put them into the casserole with the root vegetables.

7. Next add the BEEF to the frying pan and fry until it changes colour. Then add the beef to the casserole.

8. To the casserole add the mixed dried herbs, a couple of pinches of pepper, cornflour+water and the stock cubes, broken up and stir very well.

9. Place in the oven for $2^{1}/_{2}$ hours.

Ingredients

700g (1$^{1}/_{2}$ lb) stewing beef as large pieces

at least 1 kilo (2 lbs 4oz) fresh root vegetables (Choose from carrots, swedes, parsnips, sweet potato, squash, pumpkin , turnips, or buy a 1 kilo bag of fresh stew vegetables)

2 fresh onions

2 tablespoons oil

2 beef stock cubes

2 cups water

3 tablespoons cornflour

salt, pepper

1 teaspoon mixed dried herbs

1$^{1}/_{4}$ kilos (2$^{1}/_{2}$ lbs) fresh potatoes

4 cups fresh green vegetables

safety!

Use oven gloves and have heat-proof mat for the finished casserole.

Wash boards and utensils used with raw meat thoroughly in detergent and hot water and do not use for anything else until this has been done. Wash your hands after handling raw meat.

*Using fresh
vegetables?
See page 15*

*This recipe needs fresh root vegetables:
frozen ones break up and go mushy*

Needs a heat-proof oven casserole dish with lid

10. 1 hour before the casserole is due to finish, prepare the POTATOES. Peel and cut them into quarters. Just cover them with water, add $^1/_2$ teaspoon of salt, bring them to the boil, then reduce the heat and cook, bubbling gently, with a lid on the pan, for approximately 15–20 minutes until soft when tested with a fork.

11. Drain by using a colander placed over the sink. Return the potatoes to the pan and mash firmly with a potato masher until no lumps are left. Replace lid on the saucepan.

12. <u>While the potatoes are cooking</u> prepare the GREEN VEGETABLES.

13. Put them in a pan with 1 cup of water and a pinch of salt. Bring them to the boil , then reduce heat and cook, with lid on bubbling slowly, until tender when tested with the tip of a knife. Drain by using colander placed over the sink. Serve.

Also try this!

This is the basic form of a very versatile recipe. You could add either 2 tablespoons of tomato puree, 2 tablespoons of curry paste, extra dried herbs such as oregano and basil, or a little chili powder.

You may find you have some vegetables and gravy left over. Do not throw this away. Use it to make a meal for the next day. Cool, cover and refrigerate overnight and then, next day drain and rinse a tin of beans and add to the vegetables and gravy with 2 tablespoons of cornflour and 1 tablespoon of curry paste or two tablespoons of tomato puree. Heat to thicken. Serve with jacket potatoes and grated cheese and a salad.

Or thin down the gravy mixture with water, add curry paste and half a cup of red lentils, rinsed in a sieve. Cook for 15–20 minutes until the lentils are softened. Season and serve as soup.

HOT BEEF CURRY
with jacket potatoes

Preparation

Preheat oven to 180ºC (350ºF)

1. If you are using any fresh vegetables prepare them now.

2. If you are using fresh coriander, wash and chop it on a board or cut it with scissors.

3. Check the POTATOES for dirt. Cut out any bad blemishes and wash in cold water.

4. If the beef is not pre-cut, rinse it in cold water and cut into cubes, approximately 2.5cm (1") on a board.

5. Next start the BEEF CURRY by putting a large saucepan on moderate heat and adding the oil, onions, peppers and beef. Fry, stirring, until the onions are softened and the beef has changed colour.

6. Add the curry paste and stir well.

7. Add the coconut milk, carrots, a good pinch of pepper, water and the stock cube, broken up. Mix well.

8. Bring to the boil.

9. Transfer to the casserole.

10. Put the lid on the casserole and

Ingredients

700g (1$^1/_2$ lbs) stewing beef, preferably pre-cut into cubes

2 cups onions, fresh or frozen, sliced or diced

1 cup frozen sliced peppers

1 cup frozen carrots

1 cup tinned coconut milk, or reduced fat coconut milk

beef stock cube

3 tablespoons hot curry paste

$^1/_2$ cup water

2 tablespoons oil

salt, pepper

4 baking potatoes

4 cups vegetables, frozen or fresh.

2 tablespoons chopped coriander, fresh or frozen

Using fresh vegetables?
See page 15

Needs a heat-proof oven casserole dish with lid

place the casserole in the oven for 1¹/₂ hours. <u>Place the potatoes in the oven at the same time.</u>

11. <u>After the casserole has been in the oven</u> for 1¹/₄ hours cook the VEGETABLES.

12. Put the vegetables in a saucepan and add 1 cup cold water and a pinch of salt.

13. Bring to the boil, then reduce heat and cook, bubbling gently, with a lid on the pan for about 5–10 minutes until the vegetables are just tender when tested with the point of a knife. Drain by using a colander placed in the sink.

14. When the beef has been cooking for 1¹/₂ hours, check everything is cooked, add the coriander and serve.

Safety!

Use oven gloves

Have heat proof mat for the casserole when it is finished

Wash boards and all utensils used with raw meat very thoroughly in detergent and hot water and do not use for anything else until this has been done. Wash your hands after handling raw meat.

Also try this!

Although I think that casseroling meat in the oven gives a better result, this recipe can be cooked on top of the cooker in a saucepan.

Omit pre-heating the oven and follow the instructions to stage 8. Cook, bubbling gently, for 1¹/₂ hours, with a lid on the saucepan, stirring occasionally. Serve with rice or mashed potatoes.

YIPEE CHILI
with rice

Preparation

1. Open the tin of kidney beans, drain in a sieve and rinse.

2. If you are using any fresh vegetables, prepare them now.

3. To start the CHILI put the oil in a large saucepan on moderate heat, add the onions and fry until well softened.

4. Add the garlic, chili powder, oregano and cumin and stir well.

5. Add the beef mince, breaking up any big pieces with a wooden spoon and fry until it changes colour.

6. Add the tinned tomatoes, beef stock cubes, broken up and tomato puree. Stir well.

7. Add the beans to the saucepan.

8. Cook, gently bubbling, with lid on, stirring occasionally, for 30 minutes.

9. <u>As soon as the beef is cooking</u>, start the RICE. See p. 44.

10. <u>While the rice is cooking</u>, start the VEGETABLES.

11. Place the vegetables in a saucepan with 1 cup of water and a little salt.

Ingredients

450g (1 lb) beef mince

2 cups onions, frozen or fresh, sliced or diced

garlic: either two cloves fresh, peeled and crushed or 1 teaspoon garlic in oil or 1 teaspoon frozen

$1/2$ teaspoon chili powder (this will be mild – if you like it stronger, taste before it is totally cooked and add more)

2 teaspoons dried oregano

1 teaspoon dried ground cumin

1 large tin chopped tomatoes

2 tablespoons tomato puree

2 tablespoons oil

2 beef stock cubes

large tin kidney beans

4 cups vegetables frozen or fresh

salt, pepper

225g (8 oz) $1^1/_4$ cups long grain rice

**Using fresh
vegetables?
See page 15**

12. Bring to the boil, then turn down the heat and cook, gently bubbling, with the lid on for approximately 5-10 minutes until they are tender when tested with the point of a knife.

13. Drain by using a colander placed in the sink.

14. Check seasoning in chili. Serve.

Chili is a very useful recipe. Use it for filling tortillas, savoury pancakes or Staffordshire oatcakes. Cover with white or cheese sauce. Cook in the oven for 30 minutes at 180°C (350°F).

safety!

Wash boards and all utensils used for raw meat well in detergent and hot water and do not use for anything else until this is done. Wash your hands after handling raw meat.

WHITE SAUCE

Put 275ml (¹/₂ pint) milk, 1 tablespoon conflour, ¹/₂ tablespoon butter or margarine in a saucepan (preferably non-stick). Mix well. Place on a medium heat and stir until thickened. Add seasoning.

Add cheese if wished.

Also try this!

Add two cups frozen carrots to the chili at the same time as the beans and forget about separate vegetables.

Add two cups of frozen peppers, with the onions, for a Tex Mex flavour.

Serve with tortilla chips.

SHEPHERD'S PIE
and vegetables

Preparation

Preheat oven to 180°C (350°F)

1. If you are using any fresh vegetables prepare them now.

2. Peel the potatoes and cut into small pieces, about 4cm (1$\frac{1}{2}$") in size. Put in a pan and cover with cold water. Add a little salt. Set aside.

3. Mix the cornflour into the water.

4. Put the oil in a saucepan and fry the onions on a moderate heat until well softened.

5. Add the BEEF MINCE and fry until slightly browned, breaking up any lumps with a wooden spoon.

6. Add the water+cornflour and the stock cube broken up, then add the carrots.

7. Bring to the boil, then turn down the heat and cook, gently bubbling, with a lid on the pan, for about 30 minutes, stirring occasionally.

8. As soon as the beef is cooking start to cook the POTATOES.

9. Bring the pan of potatoes to the boil, then reduce the heat and cook gently, with a lid on, for about 15-20 minutes until the potatoes

Ingredients

450g (1 lb) beef mince

2 tablespoons oil

onions: 2 cups frozen or fresh, sliced or diced,

2 cups carrots frozen or fresh, diced

1 beef stock cube

2 tablespoons cornflour

2 cups water

1 tablespoon margarine or butter

small amount milk, for potato topping

approximately 1.25 kilos (2$\frac{1}{2}$ lb) fresh potatoes

4 cups vegetables, frozen or fresh

salt, pepper

safety!

Use oven gloves.

Place dish on a heatproof mat when it comes out of the oven.

Wash boards and all utensils used with raw meat very thoroughly in detergent and hot water and do not use for anything else until this has been done. Wash your hands after handling raw meat.

*Using fresh
vegetables?
See page 15*

Needs a heat-proof oven dish at least 22cm square

are soft when tested with a fork.

10. Drain using a colander placed in the sink.

11. Replace the potatoes in the pan and mash, with a potato masher, until all the lumps have been removed.

12. Add the margarine or butter and a little milk and mix with wooden spoon to make a soft mixture.

13. <u>When the mince is cooked</u> place it in the ovenproof dish and spoon the potato on top. Even it out and make a pattern if feeling creative!

14. Place the pie in the oven for 15–20 minutes until the top is browned.

I always put a large metal oven sheet under the pie in case it bubbles over.

15. <u>When the pie is in the oven</u>, start the VEGETABLES.

16. Place the vegetables in a saucepan on medium heat, add one cup of cold water and a little salt.

17. Bring to the boil. Turn down the heat and cook, with a lid on the pan, for 5–10 minutes until tender when tested with the tip of a knife. Drain by using a colander placed in the sink.

19. Serve.

Also try this!

Add one or two cups frozen peas when you add the carrots.

Spread a tin of baked beans over the mince before putting the potato topping on

Use dried potato instead of cooking fresh.

Add tablespoon curry paste to the meat mixture.

Jazz up the mash with garlic, grated cheese or mustard.

MEXICAN MINCE
with rice

Preparation

1. If you are using any fresh vegetables, prepare them now.

2. Drain and rinse the kidney beans.

3. Mix the cornflour into the water.

4. To cook the MINCE put the oil in a saucepan on a medium heat and then add the mince.

5. Fry the mince, breaking up the lumps with a wooden spoon, until it has changed colour.

6. Add the chili powder, cinnamon and oregano and stir well.

7. Add the water+cornflour mixture. Mix well. Add the tomato puree.

8. Add the kidney beans, almonds and raisins and stock cube, broken up. Stir well.

9. Cook, bubbling slowly, without the lid on the pan, for 30 minutes, stirring from time to time.

10. As soon as the mince is cooking start the RICE. See page 44.

11. When the mince has been cooking for 15 minutes start the VEGETABLES by putting them into a saucepan with 1 cup of cold water and a pinch of salt.

Ingredients

450g (1 lb) beef mince

4 tablespoons tomato puree

1 beef stock cube

2 tablespoons oil

$1/2$ teaspoon chili powder

2 teaspoons oregano

$1/4$ teaspoon cinnamon

50g (2oz) raisins

50g (2 oz) flaked almonds

1 tablespoon cornflour

1 cup water

225g(8oz) $1^1/4$ cups long grain rice

large tin kidney beans.

4 cups vegetables, frozen or fresh

Salt, pepper

40

Using fresh
vegetables?
See page 15

12. Bring the vegetables to the boil, and then reduce the heat and cook, bubbling slowly, with a lid on the saucepan, for approximately 5–10 minutes until just tender when tested with the point of a knife. Drain by using a colander placed in the sink.

13. When everything is ready, check the mince seasoning and serve.

safety!

Wash all boards and utensils used with raw meat very thoroughly in hot water and detergent. Wash your hands after handling raw meat.

Also try this!

The mince can either be used as the base for a Shepherd's Pie, or to fill tortillas or wraps. Jazz the wraps up with low fat Greek yoghurt and guacamole, or pour white or cheese sauce on top and bake at 180ºC (350ºF) for 30 minutes (see page 109 for how to make white sauce).

Add two cups of sweetcorn when the mince has been cooking for 15 minutes.

CURRIED CHICKEN AND ALMONDS

Preparation

1. If you are using any fresh vegetables, prepare them now.

2. Mix the cornflour into the water.

3. Wash and chop the coriander on a board, or cut with kitchen scissors.

4. Rinse the CHICKEN BREASTS in cold water and cut downwards onto a board, into cubes of approximately 2.5cm (1").

5. Put the oil into a large frying pan on the stove on medium heat and add the onion. Fry until the onion is softened and just starting to brown.

6. Add the chicken and peppers and fry until the chicken changes colour.

7. Add the curry paste, ground almonds, water+cornflour and the stock cube, broken up and stir well.

8. Bring to the boil. Then reduce the heat and cook, bubbling gently, with a lid on the pan, for about 20 minutes, stirring occasionally. After 20 minutes turn off the heat and pull the pan to one side. Keep it covered until the rice is ready.

9. As soon as the chicken is cooking,

Ingredients

4 boneless skinless chicken breasts

2 cups onions, fresh or frozen, sliced or diced

2 cups frozen sliced peppers

4 tablespoons curry paste

2 tablespoons oil

2 cups water

2 tablespoons cornflour

chicken stock cube

2 tablespoons ground almonds

2 tablespoons flaked almonds (preferably toasted)

4 tablespoons crème fraiche or reduced fat crème fraiche

salt, pepper

225g (8 oz) 1$^1/_4$ cups long grain rice

fresh coriander

4 cups vegetables, frozen or fresh.

*Using fresh
vegetables?
See page 15*

---

start the RICE see p. 44.

10. <u>When the rice is cooking</u>, cook the VEGETABLES

11. Put the vegetables into a pan with 1 cup water and a pinch of salt. Bring to the boil, then reduce heat and cook, covered, bubbling gently for 5-10 minutes until tender when tested with the point of a knife. Drain by using a colander placed in the sink.

12. To finish the chicken, stir in the crème fraiche and scatter the coriander and flaked almonds over the top. Check it is warm, but do not boil.

safety!

Wash boards and all utensils used with raw meat very thoroughly in hot water and detergent and do not use for anything else until this has been done. Wash your hands after handling raw meat.

OLD-FASHIONED CHICKEN POT ROAST

Preparation

1. Prepare the root vegetables. Cut them into largish chunks.

2. Place the vegetables into a large pan (with lid) with the water, stock cubes, broken up, 2 pinches of pepper and the mixed dried herbs.

3. Prepare the onions. Fry them with the oil until they are well softened. Put them in the saucepan with the root vegetables. Mix all well.

4. Cut the string or elastic from the chicken and remove it. Rinse the chicken well inside and out with cold water. Although not strictly necessary, I cut off the skin and fat at the back of the cavity under the legs, the loose skin at the front of the breast, and the "parsons nose", the bit that sticks out at the tail end. Use a sharp knife with care. Cutting these bits off gives an open bird that cooks a bit faster. Do not tie the legs back into the chicken.

5. Put the chicken in the saucepan amongst the vegetables.

6. Bring to the boil, then turn down the heat and put the lid on the pan and cook, bubbling very gently, for $1^1/_2$ hours.

Ingredients

1 oven ready fresh chicken approximately 1.5 kilos (3$^1/_2$ lbs)

at least 1 kilo (2 lbs 4oz) fresh root vegetables (choose from carrots, swedes, parsnips, sweet potato, squash, pumpkin , turnips, or buy a 1 kilo bag of fresh stew vegetables)

2 onions

2 tablespoons oil

1.25 kilos (2$^1/_2$ lbs) fresh potatoes

2 chicken stock cubes

2 teaspoons mixed dried herbs

3 tablespoons cornflour

2 cups water.

4 cups of green vegetables, frozen or fresh

salt, pepper

safety!

Wash all utensils used with chicken well in hot water and detergent and do not use for anything else until this has been done.

Wash your hands after handling raw chicken.

*Using fresh
vegetables?
See page 15*

*This recipe needs fresh root vegetables:
frozen ones break up and go mushy*

8. <u>After the chicken has been cooking
for 45 minutes</u> prepare the potatoes. Peel and cut each potato into
4 pieces. Place into a pan and just
cover with cold water and $1/2$ teaspoon salt. Bring to the boil. Turn
down the heat and cook, bubbling
gently, with a lid on the pan for 20
minutes until they are tender
when tested with the tip of a knife.

9. Drain using a colander placed in
the sink. Return the potatoes to
the pan, and mash firmly with a
potato masher until there are no
lumps left. Replace the lid on the
pan, and leave on one side until
everything else is ready.

10. <u>While the potatoes are cooking</u>
cook the vegetables by placing
them in a saucepan with 1 cup of
water and a pinch of salt. Bring to
the boil. Turn down the heat and
cook, bubbling gently, for 5–10 minutes until tender when tested with
the tip of a knife.

11. Drain using a colander placed in
the sink. Return the vegetables to
the pan and replace the lid.

12. Mix the cornflour into a little
water and add to the chicken in the
pan. Stir until it thickens. Serve.

Also try this!

*Add fresh a few sprigs herbs,
parsley, coriander, rosemary or
basil to the casserole.*

Cook the casserole in the oven

*Preheat the oven to 160°C
(320°F) and place all the vegetables and the chicken into a
large heatproof oven casserole
exactly as instructed for the
stove top version, except mix
the cornflour into the water
when adding it. Put the lid on
and cook for 2 hours*

*After 1 hour 15 minutes, start
the potatoes and vegetables.*

*The longer oven cooking is well
worthwhile if you have time.*

QUICK CHICK

Preparation

Preheat oven to 180°C (350°F)

1. Rinse the chicken. (I cut any spare loose bits of skin off with kitchen scissors. It isn't essential but it does look nicer.)

2. Peel the potatoes and cut into cubes of approximately 2.5cm (1").

3. Put the oil in a cup or bowl. Brush all the surfaces of the potatoes with oil using a pastry brush.

4. Brush the bottom of both roasting tins with oil.

5. Place the CHICKEN and POTATOES in the roasting tins. <u>The potatoes should be in a single layer and not crowded together or they will not get brown.</u> Pour any remaining oil over the potatoes.

6. Sprinkle 1 teaspoon salt over the potatoes and place both tins in the oven.

7. Cook for 45 minutes, turning the potatoes at least once.

8. The potatoes and chicken should be browned after 45 minutes. If they are, turn off the oven. Leave chicken and potatoes in the oven.

Ingredients

4 chicken quarters, or legs or thighs, the number according to the size.

approximately 1.5 k (3 lbs) fresh potatoes (do plenty, they shrink in cooking. Only fresh potatoes will work in this recipe)

salt, pepper

gravy granules

4–6 tablespoons oil

4 cups frozen vegetables or fresh cut small

75

9. Next cook the VEGETABLES by putting them in a saucepan with 1 cup of water and a pinch of salt. Bring to the boil, then turn down and cook, bubbling gently, with the lid on the pan for 5–10 minutes until they are just tender when tested with the tip of a knife. Drain by using a colander placed in the sink. Return to the pan while the gravy is made.

10. Prepare the gravy according to the package instructions.

11. Check everything is cooked and serve

Safety!

Use oven gloves. Have heat-proof mats ready for the finished dishes.

Check chicken is cooked through. There should be no red in the middle.

Wash all boards and equipment used with the chicken well in hot water and detergent and do not use with anything else until this has been done. Wash your hands after handling raw chicken.

Also try this!

Root vegetables such as carrots, sweet potatoes and squash can be cooked in the same way as the potatoes in this recipe, as can fresh peppers, mushrooms and onions. Wash , peel and chop, as appropriate

Cajun spice or any spicy mix (about 2 teaspoons) can be scattered over the potatoes instead of the salt.

Try brushing the topping from Chinese Salmon onto the chicken pieces before they are served.

SARAH'S CHICKEN CASSEROLE

Preparation

Preheat oven to 180°C (350°F)

1. If you are using any fresh vegetables, prepare them now.

2. Drain the sweetcorn if using tinned.

3. Mix the cornflour into the water.

4. Rinse the chicken in cold water. (I usually cut off any spare pieces of skin with kitchen scissors. This is not strictly necessary, but it does look nicer.)

5. Remove the rind and fat from the bacon and chop on a board or cut with scissors until fairly small.

6. Start the CASSEROLE by placing the onions, garlic, stew vegetables, carrots, sweetcorn, bacon, herbs and pepper into a large saucepan.

7. Add the stock cube, broken up and the water+cornflour. Bring to the boil and transfer to the casserole. Mix all well.

8. Put the chicken on top of the vegetables in the casserole.

9. Place the casserole, with the lid on, in the oven for 1 1/2 hours.

10. When the casserole has been in the

Ingredients

8 chicken thighs or 4 chicken quarters or 4 chicken legs

4 rashers bacon

onions: 2 cups fresh or frozen, sliced or diced

garlic: 2 cloves fresh, peeled and crushed or 1 teaspoon garlic in oil or 1 teaspoon frozen

2 cups carrots, frozen or fresh, peeled and cut into slices

2 cups frozen stewing vegetables

2 cups frozen sweetcorn or large tin sweetcorn

1 teaspoon mixed herbs

1 chicken stock cube

3 tablespoons cornflour

1 1/2 cups water

1/2 teaspoon pepper

225g(8oz) 1 1/4 cups long grain rice

4 cups vegetables, frozen or fresh

*Using fresh
vegetables?
See page 15*

Needs a heatproof oven casserole

---

oven for 1 hour, start the RICE, see page 44.

11. When the rice is cooking, start the VEGETABLES

12. Cook the vegetables, fresh or frozen by placing into a saucepan with 1 cup of cold water and a pinch of salt and cooking for 10-12 minutes, until tender when tested with the tip of a knife.

13. Drain by using a colander placed in the sink.

14. When everything is ready, serve.

safety!

Use oven gloves

Have heatproof mat ready for finished casserole.

Wash your hands thoroughly after handling chicken.

Wash all boards and utensils used with the chicken thoroughly in hot water and detergent and do not use for anything else until this has been done.

Also try this!

You could substitute jacket potatoes for the rice and put them in the oven at the same time as the casserole.

JESSIE'S EASIEST ROAST CHICKEN

Preparation

Preheat oven to 180ºC (350ºF).

1. Check the POTATOES are free of dirt. Cut out any serious blemishes and wash in cold water.

2. Cut the string or elastic from the chicken and remove it. Rinse the chicken well inside and out with cold water. Although not strictly necessary, I cut off the skin and fat at the back of the cavity under the legs, the loose skin at the front of the breast, and the "parsons nose", the bit that sticks out at the tail end. Use a sharp knife with care. Cutting these bits off gives an open bird that cooks a bit faster. Do not tie the legs back into the chicken.

3. Place the chicken in a roasting tin.

4. Pour the oil over the chicken and place in the oven.

5. Place the potatoes in the oven.

6. Leave both for $1^1/_2$ hours.

7. Turn off the oven. Leave the chicken and potatoes in.

8. Next make the gravy with gravy granules, according to the packet instructions. Pull to one side and leave covered.

Ingredients

1 oven ready roasting chicken (without giblets) approx 1.5k ($3^1/_2$ lb) The chicken should preferably be fresh, but if it is frozen, defrost completely.

gravy granules for chicken , approximately 5 heaped teaspoons (check on packet)

275ml (1/2 pint) boiling water

2 tablespoons oil

4 baking potatoes

4 cups frozen peas

salt

9. Next put the frozen peas in a saucepan with a little water and a pinch of salt.

10. Bring to the boil, then turn down the heat and cook at a gentle bubble, with a lid on the pan, for about 5 minutes .

11. Drain by using a colander placed in the sink.

12. Take the roasting tin with the chicken and the potatoes from the oven.

13. Check the chicken is thoroughly cooked. There should be no red in the middle. Return it to the oven and cook longer if there is.

14. Carve the chicken and serve with the peas and gravy.

safety!

Use oven gloves

Have a heatproof mat ready for the roasting tin when it comes out of the oven.

Wash all boards and utensils used with the chicken thoroughly in hot water and detergent and do not use for anything else until this has been done. Wash your hands after handling raw chicken.

Jessie said "You can't have a cookbook without roast chicken", so here it is. This recipe works because a 1$^1/_2$ kilo (3$^1/_2$lb) chicken cooks in approximately the same time as the baked potatoes. It won't work with larger or smaller birds.

Also try this!

Scatter a few fresh or dried herbs over the chicken before roasting or place some in the body cavity.

Peel some fresh garlic cloves, make small incisions with a knife tip and push the garlic cloves in.

Put half a lemon, orange or apple in the cavity, but do not stuff the chicken or it will take longer to cook.

THAI CURRY
with rice

Preparation

1. Rinse the chicken breasts in cold water.

2. Start cooking the RICE by selecting a cooking method see p. 44.

3. Next start the CHICKEN CURRY by chopping the chicken breasts on a board into 1" cubes.

4. Then put a medium pan on to the stove on moderate heat. Add the oil, then the onions and chicken and fry for 5–6 minutes.

5. Add the contents of the sachet of curry mix to the milk, mix well and add to the chicken.

6. Stir well and bring to the boil. Turn down the heat and cook gently with the pan covered, for 10 minutes, stirring occasionally.

7. Next add the VEGETABLES and cook, bubbling gently, for a further 10 minutes.

8. When both the rice and chicken are ready, serve.

Ingredients

4 boneless, skinless chicken breasts

packet Thai curry mix, green, yellow, or red

1 tablespoon oil

2 cups onions, frozen or fresh, chopped or sliced

4 cups Oriental frozen vegetables or frozen peas or both

300ml (1/2 pint) milk

salt, pepper

225g (8oz) $1^1/_4$ cups long grain rice

safety!

Wash all boards and utensils used with raw meat very thoroughly in hot water and detergent. Wash your hands after handling raw meat.

HURRY CURRY
with rice

Using fresh vegetables? See page 15

Preparation

1. Mix the cornflour into the water.

2. If you are using any fresh vegetables prepare them now.

3. Start cooking the MINCE by putting the oil in a saucepan on moderate heat and frying the onions until well softened.

4. Add the mince, breaking up the lumps with a wooden spoon, until it has changed colour.

5. Add the ginger, garlic, curry paste and tomato puree and stir well.

6. Add the water+cornflour, stock cube, broken up, and stir well.

7. Cook, bubbling slowly for 30 minutes, without a lid on the pan, stirring from time to time.

8. As soon as the mince is cooking start the RICE. See p. 44.

9. As soon as the rice is cooking add the VEGETABLES to the mince and stir well for a few minutes until the vegetables are cooked.

10. When everything is cooked, check mince seasoning and serve.

Ingredients

450g(1 lb) beef mince

1 cup onions, frozen or fresh, diced

2 tablespoons oil

garlic: 2 cloves fresh, peeled and chopped, or 1 teaspoon garlic in oil or frozen.

ginger: 1 teaspoon fresh, chopped finely or 1 teaspoon ginger in oil.

2 tablespoons cornflour

1 cup water

3 tablespoons curry paste

$^1/_2$ beef stock cube

2 tablespoons tomato puree

225g (8oz) 1$^1/_4$ cups long grain rice

salt, pepper

4 cups frozen vegetables, peas, peas and carrots or other diced vegetables

Also try this!

This would be nice with a tablespoon of chopped fresh coriander stirred in and a spoonful of yoghourt on the top.

Add a drained and rinsed tin of beans with the water to make a meal for bigger appetites.

INDIAN CHICKEN
with rice & vegetables

Preparation

1. If you are using any fresh vegetables, prepare them now.

2. Mix the cornflour into the water.

3. Wash and chop the coriander either on a board or you can use scissors to cut it.

4. Rinse the chicken breasts in cold water, then cut them on a board into 2.5cm (1") cubes.

5. Put the oil in a pan on medium heat and fry the onion and garlic until softened. Add the CHICKEN pieces and fry until the chicken changes colour.

6. Add the curry paste, tomato puree and coriander and stir well.

7. Add the water+cornflour and coconut milk and bring to the boil. Then turn the heat down and put a lid on the pan and cook, bubbling gently for 30 minutes. Stir occasionally. Check seasoning

8. If the chicken is finished before the rice, turn off the heat and pull the pan to one side, until the rice is ready.

9. As soon as the chicken is cooking start the RICE see p. 44.

Ingredients

4 boneless skinless chicken breasts

2 cups chopped onions, frozen or fresh

garlic: either 2 cloves fresh, peeled and crushed or 1 teaspoon processed in oil or 1 teaspoon frozen

3 tablespoons tomato puree

2 tablespoons curry paste

1 cup coconut milk or reduced fat coconut milk

$1/_2$ cup water

2 tablespoons oil

1 tablespoon cornflour

salt, pepper

coriander: 1 tablespoon chopped fresh or 1 tablespoon chopped frozen or 2 teaspoons freeze dried

225g (8 oz) $1^1/_4$ cups rice

4 cups vegetables, fresh or frozen

60

*Using fresh
vegetables?
See page 15*

10. <u>While the rice is cooking</u> cook the VEGETABLES.

11. Put 4 cups vegetables, one cup of cold water and a pinch of salt into a saucepan. Bring to the boil. Turn heat down and cook, covered, for 5-10 minutes until just tender when tested with the tip of a knife.

12. Drain by using a colander placed in the sink.

13. Serve when everything is ready.

safety!

Wash all boards and utensils used with raw chicken thoroughly in hot water and detergent and do not use with anything else until you have done this. Wash your hands after handling raw chicken.

Also try this!

Add 1 cup frozen peas or one tin chickpeas, drained, when cooking the chicken.

This would go well with jacket potatoes. If you want to invite your friends around to eat, add some extra vegetables and a tin of chickpeas.

MEXICAN CHICKEN
with rice & vegetables

Preparation

1. If you are using any fresh vegetables, prepare them now.

2. Mix the cornflour into the water.

3. Rinse the chicken breasts in cold water and cut each breast into four on a board.

4. Put the oil in a large saucepan on moderate heat.

5. Fry the onion until softened, then add the CHICKEN and fry until it changes colour.

6. To the saucepan add the peppers, tomatoes, raisins, coriander, cinnamon, chili powder, cloves (optional), water+ cornflour and a good pinch of pepper. Stir very well.

7. Add the stock cube, broken up and the chocolate. Stir well.

8. Bring to the boil, stirring well, then lower the heat and cook covered, bubbling very gently, for 30 minutes.

9. While the chicken is cooking, start the RICE See p. 44.

10. When the rice is cooked, turn off the heat and leave covered while you cook the VEGETABLES.

Ingredients

4 skinless, boneless chicken breasts

2 tablespoons oil

2 cups onions: frozen or fresh, diced or sliced

1 cup frozen sliced peppers

large tin chopped tomatoes

50g (2 oz) raisins

1 teaspoon dried coriander

$1/_4$ teaspoon cinnamon

$1/_2$ teaspoon dried chili powder

pinch cloves (optional)

25g (1oz) plain chocolate

1 chicken stock cube

$1^1/_2$ cups water

2 tablespoons cornflour

salt, pepper

225g (8oz) $1^1/_4$ cups long grain rice

4 cups vegetables, frozen or fresh

Using fresh
vegetables?
See page 15

11. Put the vegetables in pan with 1 cup of water. Add a pinch of salt. Bring to the boil. Turn down heat and cook, covered, bubbling gently for 5-10 minutes, or until just tender when tested with tip of a knife.

12. Drain by using a colander placed in the sink.

13. Check the chicken is ready and serve.

safety!

Wash chopping board and any utensils used with raw chicken thoroughly after use in hot water and detergent and do not use for anything else until this has been done. Wash your hands after handling raw meat.

Also try this!

Serve with naan bread instead of rice. Heat according to packet instructions.

Use this recipe (with the chicken cut into smaller pieces) for filling tortillas, savoury pancakes or Staffordshire oatcakes. Cover with white or cheese sauce (buy a packet or see the recipe on page 109) and cook in the oven for 30 minutes at 180ºC (350ºF).

MEXICAN CHICKEN ■ 129

SAUSAGE AND LENTIL STEW
with mashed potato

Preparation

1. If you are using fresh onions and garlic, prepare them now.

2. Rinse the lentils in a sieve under running water.

3. Mix the cornflour into the water.

4. Prepare the POTATOES by peeling, chopping them into quarters and placing them in a saucepan. Put in cold water just to cover, add a little salt and leave on one side.

5. To start the SAUSAGES put a saucepan on the stove on a moderate heat and add the oil.

6. Add the onions and fry gently until they are well softened.

7. Next add the sausages and fry until they are partly cooked. (They should not be wholly cooked at this stage.)

8. Add the garlic, spicy seasoning and peppers and fry gently for few minutes then add the water+cornflour and the stock cube, broken up, to the saucepan.

9. Add the lentils to the saucepan. Then add the carrots. Add a good pinch of pepper. Mix everything very thoroughly.

Ingredients

2 cups onions, frozen or fresh, sliced or diced

approximately 450 g (about 1 lb) sausages. About 2 large sausages a person. Buy as good quality as possible

3/4 cup red lentils

2 cups frozen peppers

3 cups frozen carrots

2 cups frozen peas or sweetcorn

2 teaspoons Cajun, jerk or fajita seasoning. These are all spicy seasonings

garlic;2 cloves fresh, peeled and crushed, or 1 teaspoon garlic in oil or frozen.

2 tablespoons oil

4 cups water

2 tablespoons cornflour

1 stock cube

pepper

900g (2 lbs) fresh potatoes

a little butter or margarine or milk

Using fresh
vegetables?
See page 15

10. Bring all to the boil. Turn down the heat and cook bubbling gently, with a lid on the saucepan, for about 25 minutes, stirring occasionally.

11. <u>As soon as the sausages are cooking</u> start to cook the POTATOES.

12. Bring them to the boil, then turn down the heat and cook, bubbling gently, with the lid on for 15–20 minutes until soft when tested with a fork. When they are cooked, drain them using a colander placed in the sink.

13. Return the potatoes to the pan and mash, with a potato masher, until no lumps are left.

14. Add a little margarine or butter and milk and mix with wooden spoon until smooth.

15. To complete the meal, add peas or corn to stew, check seasoning and cook for 5 minutes.

safety!

Wash chopping board and any utensils used with raw meat thoroughly after use in hot water and detergent and do not use for anything else until this has been done. Wash your hands after handling raw meat.

Also try this!

Use dried potato instead of fresh

Add a tablespoon of curry paste.

HERBY SAUSAGE CASSEROLE

Preparation

Preheat the oven to 180ºC (350ºF)

1. If you are using fresh vegetables, prepare them now.

2. Mix the cornflour with the water.

3. Put the oil in a saucepan on a medium heat. Add the onions and fry for a few minutes, until they are soft and are just starting to brown. Then add the sausages and fry for a few minutes. They should not be fully cooked at this stage.

4. Add the water+cornflour mixture and herbs to the saucepan. Then add the carrots or mixed vegetables, along with the garlic, and crumble the stock cube in as well. Bring to the boil.

5. Take the saucepan from the heat and put the contents into the casserole. Cook the casserole, <u>uncovered</u>, in the oven for approximately 45minutes.

6. When the casserole is put in the oven, check what needs to be done with the BREAD. If it is garlic bread follow the instructions on the packet. If it is regular bread, and you wish to heat it through, put it in the

Ingredients

2 cups onions, frozen or fresh, diced or chopped

approximately 450g (about 1 lb) sausages (about 8) Buy as good quality as possible.

Garlic: 2 cloves fresh, peeled and crushed or 1 teaspoon garlic in oil or 2 teaspoons frozen

1 teaspoon mixed dried herbs

1 teaspoon dried basil

1 teaspoon dried parsley

1 stock cube

2 tablespoons oil

2 cups water

2 tablespoons cornflour

4 cups frozen carrots or mixed vegetables or fresh vegetables, diced small

salt, pepper

bread or garlic bread, to serve

*Using fresh
vegetables?
See page 15*

*Needs an oven proof casserole
dish without a lid*

oven for the last 10 minutes of the
sausages cooking.

7. Check seasoning and serve.

TOMATO SALAD

A tomato salad or green salad with grapes and
pecans goes well with this.

Wash and slice the tomatoes. Mix $1/2$ teaspoon
sugar, $1/2$ teaspoon basil, fresh chopped (gives the
best flavour), frozen or dried, pinch black pepper,
$1/2$ teaspoon salt, 2 tablespoons olive oil and
1 tablespoon vinegar or lemon juice. Pour the
dressing over the sliced tomatoes.

GREEN SALAD WITH GRAPES AND PECANS

Prepare the green salad and wash the grapes (page
19). Make a salad dressing (page 14). Scatter on
some pecan nuts.

safety!

Use oven gloves

*Have a heatproof mat ready for
the finished casserole*

*Check the sausages are cooked
through. There should be no
pink in the middle*

*Wash chopping board and any
utensils used with raw meat
thoroughly after use in hot
water and detergent and do
not use for anything else until
this has been done. Wash your
hands after handling raw meat.*

Also try this!

*Add a tin of white beans,
drained and rinsed, to the
casserole with the sausages.*

Add a tin of chopped tomatoes.

*Make your own garlic bread
see the Introduction.*

SWEET AND SOUR PORK
with jacket potatoes

Preparation

Preheat oven to 180°C (350°F).

1. Prepare all the fresh vegetables you are using now.

2. Drain the tinned pineapple. Keep the juice for later. Cut the rings into pieces.

3. Mix the cornflour into the water, then add the pineapple juice, soy sauce, vinegar, tomato puree, ginger and a good pinch of pepper.

4. Check the potatoes for dirt, cut out any serious blemishes and wash in cold water.

5. Rinse the pork in cold water and cut the chops, downwards onto a board, cutting off the fat, into about 4 pieces, removing any bones. Cut the stewing pork into cubes of approximately 2.5cm (1").

6. Put the oil into a saucepan on moderate heat and fry the onion until softened. Then add the pork and garlic and fry until it changes colour.

7. Add the cornflour mixture and stir well. Add chopped pineapple.

8. Add the mushrooms, carrots and peppers and stir all very well.

Ingredients

pork: either approximately 560g (1$^1/_4$ lb) stewing pork or four pork chops

2 tablespoons oil

onion: 2 cups either frozen or fresh, sliced or diced

garlic: either 4 cloves fresh, peeled and crushed, or 2 teaspoons garlic in oil or 3 teaspoons frozen

4 cups carrots frozen or fresh, cut small

2 cups frozen peppers

2 cups frozen mushrooms

small tin pineapple rings

3 tablespoons soy sauce

ginger: either one teaspoon ginger in oil or four slices fresh ginger

1 tablespoon vinegar

1 tablespoon tomato puree

$^1/_2$ cup water

2 tablespoons cornflour

salt, pepper

4 baking potatoes

*Using fresh
vegetables?
See page 15*

---

9. Make everything hot, then place
   into the casserole. Place the lid on
   the casserole.

10. <u>Place the potatoes and the casse-
    role into the oven</u> and cook for $1^1/_2$
    hours.

safety!

Use oven gloves.

*Have heatproof oven mat ready
for finished casserole.*

*Wash chopping boards and all
utensils that have been used
with raw meat thoroughly in
detergent and hot water after
use and do not use for anything else until this has been
done. Wash your hands after
handling raw meat.*

Also try this!

*If you would prefer this with
rice, start cooking the rice, see
p. 44, when the casserole has
been cooking for 1hour.*

*This would be nice with a salad
containing some fruit. Prepare
salad leaves, fresh spinach or
lettuce. Add some sliced peeled
oranges, mandarin sections,
peeled ripe mango or pawpaw,
even tinned peaches. Scatter on
some nuts, such as pine nuts, or
seeds, such as sunflower or
pumpkin. Add a handful of
dried fruit if you wish, such as
blueberrries or cranberrries. I
like lemon flavoured oil on this
salad, but you choose what you
like.*

SOUTH AMERICAN PORK CASSEROLE

Preparation

Preheat oven to 180°C (350°F)

1. If you are using any fresh vegetables, prepare them now.

2. Mix the cornflour into the water.

3. Rinse the pork chops in cold water. Cut downwards onto a chopping board, removing the fat and bone and cutting each chop into 4 pieces.

4. Drain and rinse the beans and chickpeas.

5. Put the oil in a frying pan and fry the onions until well softened.

6. Add the PORK, garlic, cumin, chili and coriander and fry gently until the pork changes colour.

7. Put the pork in the casserole and add the water+cornflour, peppers and stock cubes, broken up. Stir all very well.

8. Last, add the beans and chickpeas. Stir.

9. Put the lid on the casserole and cook in the oven for 1 hour 15 minutes.

10. When the casserole has been cooking for forty five minutes, start

Ingredients

4 pork chops

1 tablespoon oil

1 cup onions, frozen or fresh, diced or sliced

garlic: 4 cloves fresh, peeled and crushed, or 2 teaspoons garlic in oil or 2 teaspoons frozen

1 cup frozen sliced peppers

1 teaspoon cumin

2 teaspoons dried coriander

$1/_2$ teaspoon chili powder

2 beef stock cubes

3 tablespoons cornflour

1 cup water

large tin red kidney beans

large tin chickpeas

salt, pepper

225g (8oz) $1^1/_4$ cups long grain rice

4 cups vegetables, frozen or fresh

cooking the RICE. See p. 44.

11. <u>While the rice is cooking, start cooking</u> the VEGETABLES.

12. Place the vegetables in a saucepan with 1 cup water and a pinch of salt.

13. Bring to the boil. Then reduce the heat and cook covered, bubbling gently for 5-10 minutes until tender when tested with the tip of a knife.

14. Drain by using a colander placed in the sink.

15. When the pork has been cooking for 1 hour 15 minutes, check it is cooked and serve.

safety!

Use oven gloves

Have heatproof mat ready for finished dish.

Wash chopping boards and all utensils that have been used with raw meat thoroughly in detergent and hot water after use and do not use for anything else until this has been done. Wash your hands after handling raw meat.

ORIENTAL CHICKEN
with rice

🕐 45

*Using fresh
vegetables?
See page 15*

Preparation

1. Mix the cornflour into the water.

2. If you are using any fresh vegetables, prepare them now.

3. Rinse the CHICKEN breasts in cold water and cut into cubes of about 2cm (3/4").

4. Put a large pan or frying pan with a lid on a moderate heat and add the oil, onions, peppers, ginger and fry until well softened.

5. Add the chicken and garlic and fry until the chicken changes colour.

6. Add the soy sauce and the water+ cornstarch. Stir and bring to boil.

7. Turn down the heat and cook, with a lid on the pan, bubbling gently for 15 minutes.

8. <u>As soon as the chicken is simmering,</u> start the RICE. See p. 44.

9. After the chicken has been cooking for 15 minutes, add the ORIENTAL VEGETABLES.

10. Bring to the boil, turn down the heat and simmer for 10 minutes.

11. Then pull the pan to side.

12. When the rice is ready, serve.

Ingredients

4 skinless, boneless chicken breasts

4 tablespoons soy sauce

2 cups onions, frozen or fresh, sliced or diced

2 cups frozen sliced peppers

ginger: either 2 teaspoons fresh root ginger, chopped finely, or 2 teaspoons processed ginger in oil

garlic: either 4 cloves fresh, peeled or crushed, or 2 teaspoons garlic in oil, or frozen

2 tablespoons oil

2 tablespoons cornflour

2 cups water

225g (8oz) 1$^1/_4$ cups long grain rice

salt, pepper

4 cups frozen oriental vegetables

safety!

Wash chopping board and any utensils used with raw chicken thoroughly after use in hot water and detergent and do not use for anything else until this has been done. Wash your hands after handling raw meat.

SWEET THINGS

DOUBLE CHOC CHIP COOKIES

Preparation

Preheat the oven to 180°C (350°F)

1. Grease the baking trays well by brushing them with a little margarine, or by greasing with a bit of kitchen paper rubbed in margarine.

2. Cream together the margarine and sugars until soft and creamy.

3. Add the vanilla. Mix in.

4. Add the bicarbonate and water and mix in.

5. Break the egg into a cup.

6. Beat well and add to the mixture, then mix in well.

7. Add the flour and cocoa. (Break up any lumps in the cocoa or put it through a sieve.)

8. Beat it all together well.

9. Stir in the chocolate chips.

10. Put teaspoonfuls of the mixture onto the trays. Leave plenty of room (approximately 5 cm or 2") between the spoonfuls as they will spread during cooking.

11. Place in the oven and bake for approximately 15 minutes.

Ingredients

110g (4oz) margarine

50g (2oz) soft brown sugar

75g (3oz) white sugar

1 egg

$1/2$ teaspoon bicarbonate of soda + 1 teaspoon hot water to mix

150g (5oz) plain flour

1 tablespoon cocoa powder

1x100g packet chocolate chips (in the home baking section of a supermarket)

$1/2$ teaspoon vanilla essence

**Makes approximately
20 cookies**

**Needs large metal baking
sheets, preferably two**

12. Remove from the baking sheet
    while still warm, with a fish slice or
    palette knife.

13. Cool on a wire rack. (The grilling
    rack of your grill pan will do if you
    don't have one.)

safety!

Use oven gloves

Also try this!

Naughty, naughty!

*Sandwich biscuits together with
Greek yoghurt or whipped
cream and serve with a scoop
of ice cream and washed sliced
strawberries*

*Make regular chocolate chip
cookies by substituting a tablespoon of plain flour for the
cocoa*

JESSIE'S MULTI-CHOICE CAKES

Preparation

Preheat oven to 180°C (350°F)

1. Weigh all the ingredients.

2. Grease the cake tins well either by using a pastry brush and brushing with oil or margarine or by using a bit of kitchen paper with margarine on it.

3. If you are using baking parchment or greasproof paper, cut paper to fit the base of the tin. If you use greasproof paper, either oil or grease with margarine, brushed on, or spread with a piece of kitchen roll.

4. Beat the margarine and sugar together in a bowl until soft and lighter coloured.

5. Break the eggs into another bowl and beat until smooth.

6. Mix the eggs and vanilla into the margarine and sugar and beat well.

7. Next add the self raising flour or plain flour+baking powder and beat again very thoroughly.

8. Spoon into tin or tins and even out surface.

9. Cook for 20–30 minutes according

Ingredients

WHITE CAKE

175g (6oz) soft margarine suitable for cooking (There will be a symbol on the side of the plastic tub)

175g (6oz) white sugar

175g (6oz) either self raising flour or plain flour with $1^1/_2$ teaspoons baking powder added.

3 eggs

1 teaspoon vanilla

This started off as Jessie's White Cake, but has developed into a whole range of easy cakes

Each cake needs either two round sponge cake tins, approximately 18cm (7") or one rectangular tin approximately 18cmX 28cm (7" X 11 ")

to thickness. The two round tins will take about 20 minutes, the rectangular tin will take 25-30 minutes.

10. The cake is cooked when it is lightly browned evenly and springs back when gently pressed with a finger.

11. Let it cool a little and then turn out onto cooling rack. (If you do not have a cooling rack, use a grill rack.)

12. When cool, sandwich together with jam and decorate with butter icing or water icing.

13. A cake cooked in two tins makes a classic birthday cake when decorated.

FOLLOW THE BASIC INSTRUCTIONS
FOR WHITE CAKE TO MAKE ALL
THE VARIATIONS ON PAGES 144-145.

Butter Icing

Beat 50g (2oz) margarine and 3 teaspoons of milk with 225g (8oz) icing sugar (which should be sieved to get out any lumps). Beat well with a fork to initially mash the icing sugar and margarine together and then beat with a spoon to get a smooth texture. This will fill the centre and cover the top of two round sponges or cover the top of one oblong cake.

Halve the amount if you are just filling the middle.

Water Icing

Put 110g (4oz) icing sugar, (sieved if lumpy) with 4 teaspoons of water. Mix well. Spread on cake and allow to dry. This will cover the top of one round sponge. Double the amount for the rectangular cakes.

Chocolate cake

Weigh only 150g (5oz) flour and add 25g (1oz) cocoa powder. Cook as White Cake above.

To make a chocolate topping, melt Chocolate Flavoured Cake Topping over a pan of simmering water.

Topping chocolate usually comes in large squares, in which case the round cake takes 4 squares and the rectangular cake, 8 squares.

If making a round sandwich cake, the middle can be filled with butter icing with a tablespoon of drinking chocolate powder added.

Fruit cake

Add 225g (8oz) of any dried fruit to the mixture in the final mixing. This is better cooked in a rectangular tin and does not need icing. Add a teaspoon of dried mixed spice if you wish.

Lemon cake

Wash the lemon very well and grate the rind finely. Squeeze the juice into a bowl and set aside.

Put the lemon rind into the cake on the final mixing.

While the cake is in the oven, put 3 tablespoons of sugar into the lemon juice and stir.

As soon as the cake comes out of the oven, brush, spoon or pour the lemon juice mixture all over the top and allow to cool.

Orange Cake

Same as Lemon Cake but use an orange instead.

Cherry Cake

Add 110g (4oz) glace cherries to the final mixing.

Coffee and Pecan Cake

Mix 2 teaspoons of instant coffee powder with 1 tablespoon of hot water. Add to the final mix of the cake, along with approximately 50g (2 oz) of chopped pecans. Mix well.

Add a little instant coffee to the water icing for the top and fill the middle with butter icing if making a sandwich cake.

Mosaic Cake

Make the basic white cake mix and divide into two. Put into separate bowls. Into one bowl add 1 tablespoon cocoa powder and mix well. Leave the other half white. Into the cake tin, put large tablespoons of alternate chocolate and white mix. Next stir with a thin kitchen tool, such as knife blade, fork or kebab stick, to roughly mix them and produce the marble effect.

Ice with chocolate flavoured topping (see chocolate cake).

Another variation on this would be to scrub and finely grate an orange and add the grated peel to the bowl of white cake mix to make a chocolate and orange cake.

Little buns

Buy some paper bun cases and place on flat metal baking trays. Fill with heaped teaspoons of any of the mixtures and cook for about 10–15 minutes.

These are good for children's parties iced with water icing and decorated with sprinkles.

LUTHIEN'S FLAPJACK

Preparation

Preheat the oven to 180ºC (350ºF)

1. Break the egg into a cup and beat well.

2. Grease thoroughly a baking tin by brushing well with oil.

3. Cut baking parchment to fit base of tin, or at a pinch, use greaseproof paper, well brushed with oil.

4. Put sugar, butter or margarine and the golden syrup in a pan and heat gently.

5. When the sugar, syrup and butter or margarine have just melted, remove the saucepan from the heat and stir in the porridge oats, vanilla and egg. Mix very thoroughly.

6. Put the mixture evenly into the baking tin. Smooth down. Cook in the oven for 20–25 minutes, until lightly browned and starting to go darker at the edges.

7. Put the tin on a cooling tray for a few minutes.

8. Then mark the flapjack into pieces, but do not finally cut and remove from tin until almost cold.

Ingredients

110g (4oz) Demerara sugar
110g (4 oz) butter or margarine
175g (6oz) porridge oats
3 tablespoons golden syrup
1 teaspoon vanilla essence
1 egg

To measure the syrup, use a metal tablespoon and dip in hot water before measuring it. This makes it easier.

Baking parchment is necessary to line the base of the tin, otherwise it is hard to get the flapjack from the tin and it breaks up. This needs a wire cooling rack (use grill rack if you don't have a cooling rack)

CELEBRATIONS

Three courses are, by my standards, a celebration – but three courses are very difficult to co-ordinate. These two menus allow the first and last courses to be made earlier and kept covered in the fridge until it is time to eat, allowing the cook to produce all three courses at the same time, impress everyone and accept the congratulations graciously...

CELEBRATION MENU 1
Prawn cocktail
Chicken in White Wine Sauce
Lemon meringues

CELEBRATION Menu 2
Pate plate
Gingered beef casserole
Chocolate mousse

25

PRAWN COCKTAIL

Preparation

1. Defrost the prawns by placing into cold water.

2. When defrosted, drain well.

3. Mix the prawns with the seafood sauce.

4. Arrange the salad in small bowls, plates, saucers or drinking glasses.

5. Put the prawn mixture equally on top of the salads.

6. Decorate.

7. Cover with cling film and refrigerate.

8. At the last minute add either the crackers or the buttered bread quarters.

Ingredients

small packet frozen, cooked, peeled prawns

jar seafood sauce approximately 180g (6 oz)

4 or 8 savoury crackers, or two slices of buttered bread cut into quarters

small packet washed salad

decorations: quarter slices of tomato, cucumber or orange or a blob of mayonnaise

CHICKEN IN WHITE WINE SAUCE

🕐 60

Using fresh vegetables? See page 15

Preparation

1. If you are using any fresh vegetables prepare them now.

2. Wash the potatoes and check for dirt. Put them in a saucepan with a pinch of salt and just cover with cold water. Leave aside for a short while.

3. To start cooking the CHICKEN rinse the chicken breasts and cut them downwards onto a board into approximately 2.5cm (1") cubes.

4. Then put the butter or margarine into a saucepan on medium heat and add the onions. Gently fry the onions until well softened.

5. Add the chicken pieces and fry for 3–4 minutes until the chicken changes colour. Add the mushrooms and cook for a further 1–2 minutes.

6. Add the contents of the wine sauce packet into 300ml ($^1/_2$ pint) milk (or according to the instructions) and add to the pan and stir well.

7. Bring to the boil, then turn down the heat and cook gently, with a lid on the pan, for 15 minutes.

Ingredients

4 skinless boneless chicken breasts cut into 1" cubes.

packet Chicken in White Wine Sauce mix

2 cups onions, fresh or frozen, sliced or chopped

2 cups frozen mushrooms

25g (1oz) butter or margarine

275ml (1/2 pint) milk (see wine sauce packet instructions)

approx 450g (1 lb) new potatoes

packet mange tout peas, or prepared baby beans

salt pepper

CHICKEN IN WHITE WINE SAUCE

8. Turn off the heat and put the chicken saucepan to one side.

9. <u>As soon as the chicken is bubbling,</u> cook the POTATOES. Bring them to the boil and then reduce heat and cook, bubbling gently, with a lid on the pan, for about 15 minutes, until they are tender when tested with the point of a knife.

10. Drain by using a colander placed in the sink. Return the potatoes to the pan.

11. <u>Five minutes before the potatoes are due to finish,</u> put the VEGETABLES into saucepan with 1 cup of water and a pinch of salt. Bring to the boil. Then turn down heat and cook gently for approximately 4 minutes. Drain by using a colander placed in the sink.

12. Check the chicken is warm enough and serve.

safety!

Wash boards and utensils used with raw meat thoroughly in hot water and detergent. Do not use for any other food until this has been done. Wash your hands after handling raw meat.

5

LEMON MERINGUES

Preparation

1. Mix the lemon curd with the Mascarpone.

2. Taste and add more lemon curd if it is not lemony enough.

3. Divide between the meringues.

4. Sprinkle on the grated chocolate.

5. Cover with cling film and refrigerate.

Ingredients

250g tub Mascarpone cheese

4 large tablespoons lemon curd

packet individual meringues (usually has 8 in it)

grated chocolate, to decorate

This makes 8 meringues.

Most people I know can eat two each, but if this seems too much, halve the recipe and keep the meringues in an air tight container for another time.

⏱ 15

PATE PLATE

Preparation

1. Arrange the salad on 4 small plates.

2. Cut the pate into quarters and place each in the middle of a salad.

3. Decorate.

4. Cover with cling film and refrigerate.

5. At the last minute add either the crackers or the buttered bread quarters.

Ingredients

packet of pate, any one you like, approx 170g (6oz)

small packet washed salad

4 or 8 savoury crackers, or 2 slices of buttered bread cut into quarters

decorations: quarter slices of tomato, cucumber, orange or a blob of mayonnaise

GINGERED BEEF CASSEROLE

with new potatoes

Needs a heat-proof oven casserole with lid

Preparation

Preheat the oven to 160°C (320°F)

1. Check the potatoes for dirt. Wash them and put them into a saucepan with cold water just to cover. Add $1/_2$ teaspoon salt.

2. If you are using any fresh vegetables prepare them now.

3. Mix the cornflour into the water.

4. Rinse the beef if not pre-cut and cut into cubes on a chopping board.

5. Put the oil into a large frying pan on moderate heat and add the BEEF and chili powder. Fry gently until the beef changes colour.

6. Place the beef in the casserole.

7. To the casserole add the tomatoes, tomato puree, ginger, garlic, mushrooms, vinegar, sugar, Worcestershire sauce, water + cornflour and stock cube, broken up. Stir well.

8. Place the casserole, with the lid on, in the oven for 2 hours.

9. When the meat has been cooking for $1^1/_2$ hours cook the POTATOES.

10. Bring to the boil then reduce the

Ingredients

675g ($1^1/_2$ lb) stewing beef preferably pre-cut into cubes

3 tablespoons oil

1 large tin chopped tomatoes

2 tablespoons tomato puree

2 teaspoons ground dried ginger

$1/_2$ teaspoon chili powder

2 cups frozen sliced mushrooms

1 tablespoon Worcestershire sauce

1 tablespoon dark brown sugar

2 tablespoons vinegar, preferably wine vinegar

2 cloves fresh garlic, peeled and crushed or 1 teaspoon garlic in oil or frozen

beef stock cube

$1/_2$ cup water

2 tablespoons cornflour

pepper

approximately 700g ($1^1/_2$ lb) new potatoes

4 cups interesting vegetables, for instance baby carrots, julienne carrots, fine green beans, mange tout, or broccoli and cauliflower mixture, frozen or fresh

GINGERED BEEF CASSEROLE

heat and cook, gently bubbling, with a lid on the pan for about 15 minutes. Drain by using a colander placed in the sink.

11. <u>Next</u> cook the VEGETABLES.

12. Place fresh or frozen vegetables in a saucepan with 1 cup of water and a pinch of salt.

13. Bring to the boil, turn down heat and cook with lid on for 5–10 minutes until tender. Drain by using a colander placed in the sink.

14. When everything is ready, serve.

safety!

Wash boards and utensils used with raw meat thoroughly in hot water and detergent. Do not use for any other food until this has been done. Wash your hands after handling raw meat.

Use oven gloves

Have heatproof mat ready for finished casserole.

Also try this!

Add a large tin drained, rinsed kidney beans to casserole at the same time as the tin of tomatoes.

Add 6 chopped sun dried tomatoes in oil, or olives, 10 minutes before the casserole is finished.

CHOCOLATE MOUSSE

Preparation

1. Wash the orange and grate 1 teaspoon of rind.

2. Squeeze the juice and measure 2 tablespoonfuls into a bowl.

3. Put a pan of hot water onto a low heat, with a heat-proof basin placed inside it.

4. Break up the chocolate and melt it in this basin over the pan of hot water.

5. When melted, mix the chocolate with the Quark, orange rind, juice and vanilla essence.

6. Divide between 4 small bowls, glasses or cups.

7. Cool.

8. When cool enough put a layer of yoghourt on the top of each mousse.

9. Decorate with grated chocolate.

10. Cover with cling film and refrigerate until ready to eat.

Ingredients

250g pot Quark
110g (4oz) dark chocolate
1 orange
1teaspoon vanilla essence
vanilla yoghourt or sweetened Greek yoghourt
grated chocolate to decorate

INDEX